ERNEST HEMINGWAY AND THE LITTLE MAGAZINES

ERNEST HEMINGWAY AND THE LITTLE MAGAZINES: *THE PARIS YEARS*

by NICHOLAS JOOST

BARRE PUBLISHERS - BARRE, MASSACHUSETTS 1968

FOR LAURA

CONTENTS

EPIGRAPH

The small magazines and the small publishing houses — how would authorship fare without them? The big firms . . . are on the look-out for budding talent. But they cannot devote to apprentice work the attention which the young writer needs. A writer is self-taught. He teaches himself by writing. He needs to see himself in print. Until he does, he cannot judge himself, cannot assess himself. He needs to talk his work over with his contemporaries. The young must have something in print to show each other. That is how they become writers. And how can they do that without the small magazines, without the small publishers? Literature stands in the debt of those who give the young that opportunity.

— Alec Waugh

CHAPTER I

THE dark, mustached young man looked out the window of his cheap walk-up flat — there it was, the whole scene captured in the smudged glass span, the river and the city of himself and his beloved, and the island of their city. . . . Life had seemed so simple to him that morning when he had wakened and had found the false spring and had heard the pipes of the man with a herd of goats and had leapt downstairs into the brisk air and had bought a racing paper. But, as Ernest Hemingway had just learned, Paris was a very old city; nothing was simple there, not even poverty nor sudden money nor the moonlight, not even the right and wrong of living.

Perhaps the most complex, the most ambiguous problem of those years of the early 1920's — as Hemingway recalled them in *A Moveable Feast* — was realizing his potentiality as a writer and enforcing the authority of his style, his perceptions upon editors and readers. Seemingly, Hemingway rose to fame as a short-story writer and novelist with the ease and power that physically he emanated in those days; but the reality was a hard struggle. For most of the time between the end of 1921, when he left Chicago for Europe, and the end of 1926, when he established himself with *The Sun Also Rises,* Hemingway led a double life. He alternated between America and Europe; in Europe, he alternated between Paris, with its river and bridges and crowded cafés, and the village of Schruns, high up in the snowy Vorarlberg where one skied; and as a writer, Hemingway alternated between journalism —at which he was more than competent, earning good money by describing Balkan wars and peace conferences for the *Toronto Star* — and writing-for-its-own-sake — at which as a beginner he was sometimes less than competent. Journalism for the *Star* he could write anywhere under any circumstances, and he worked as a reporter merely to make money to support his new wife and Mr. Bumby, their baby. The journalism also paid for those trips to Schruns, and it might be that away from Paris he could write about Paris as in Paris he could write about his boyhood in Michigan, before his trauma of the first World War. His optimism was justified but a little premature, since he did not know Paris well enough in those early months of their meeting, the months of his early married life. But eventually the Paris that captivated the young husband and wife was captured by him, in the still amber of words, in such books as *The Sun Also Rises* and *A Moveable Feast,* children of a love affair lasting forty years.

Paris: there it was, Baudelaire's *cité fourmillante,* that Ernest Hemingway learned the lessons of his craft. Paris: *ouvert la nuit* (in Paul Morand's phrase) for the first hectic, uncertain seasons of the peace; Paris, where the *poivrottes* of the Café des Amateurs, that cesspool of the Rue Mouffetard, stayed drunk on cheap wine all of the time or all of the time they could afford it; Paris, where below the Pont Neuf the statue of Henri Quatre guarded a point like the sharp bow of a ship, a little park at the Seine's edge shadowed by chestnut trees, huge and spreading, above the currents and back waters the river made flowing past, the best fishing spots for those dacelike fish called *goujon.* Hemingway ate them *en friture,* by the plateful. Paris: most significantly, where Hemingway met the friends and advisors from whom he learned so much in those years, 1922 through 1925 — Ezra Pound, Gertrude Stein, Sylvia Beach, Ford Madox Ford, Ernest Walsh, Gilbert Seldes, George Antheil, Jules Pascin,

Malcolm Cowley; and, at the close, Scott Fitzgerald to lead Hemingway away from the Latin Quarter, the Café du Dôme, the vicissitudes of publishing like the rest of the vanguard in the little magazines with their unrenumerated courage.

The story begins shortly before Hemingway's arrival in Paris in December 1921. From October 1920 until early 1921, he worked in Chicago as associate editor of *Co-operative Commonwealth,* the trade paper for an enterprise ruinously shady albeit impressively titled the Co-operative Society of America. After leaving that job, he precariously supported himself for the rest of 1921 by writing seven articles for the *Star Weekly,* the magazine adjunct of the *Toronto Star.* He submitted stories to the pulp magazine for men, *Argosy,* without success. Although he lacked a steady job, Hemingway married Hadley Richardson in Petoskey, Michigan, on September 3, 1921, and brought her back to Chicago. It was then that his postwar literary beginnings, on the fringe of the advanced artistic group of Chicago, coalesced with his journalistic work.

In Chicago that fall, Hemingway made friends with Sherwood Anderson, then at the height of his renown as a leader of the New Movement in the arts, and consequently in a position to be helpful to young men beginning as writers. That fall, also, Hemingway was enabled to earn his living in Europe, and there to develop his talent, by landing a job as roving correspondent for the *Star* in Europe, with Paris as his headquarters. Fortunately, Sherwood Anderson had just returned, in August, to Chicago from a trip to Europe, taken on the generous invitation of Paul Rosenfeld, the writer of the monthly "Musical Chronicle" in *The Dial,* and thus was fresh from meeting the very men and women who might be helpful to Hemingway in Europe.

In the fall of 1921, moreover, Anderson's leadership of the younger and more advanced American writers was recognized when he became the recipient of the first of the annual awards made by *The Dial* throughout the 1920's. Refurbished in January 1920 from a politically orientated fortnightly into a literary and artistic monthly of enlightened and advanced tastes, *The Dial* by 1921 had no serious rival in America. Its two young proprietors, Scofield Thayer and James Sibley

Watson, Jr., respectively the Editor and Publisher, decided
further to aid needy writers by establishing an annual award
— no prize, they emphasized — of two thousand dollars, to be
bestowed not for any single work by the recipient but rather
for the range and promise of his writing. As Editor, Thayer
had favored E. A. Robinson over Anderson at first, and only
by the middle of October 1921 did he agree with Watson
that Anderson should be given the award, because of his age
in part — forty-five years as against Robinson's fifty-two —
but also because Anderson was definitely of the younger
group of writers. From its first year, he had published such
stories as "I'm a Fool" and "The Triumph of the Egg" in
The Dial, and by the very fact of that publication the
magazine was widely presumed to support Anderson's leadership of the writers seeking to change the substance, tone,
and outlook of American letters. During the third week of
October 1921, Sherwood Anderson accepted the proffered
award from the Managing Editor of *The Dial,* Gilbert Seldes,
and it was understood that Paul Rosenfeld, who was close
to and sympathetic with Anderson, would write the eulogy
for the occasion, the January 1922 issue of *The Dial.*

On November 28, 1921, when Anderson wrote to Lewis
Galantière in Paris, he began his letter with an introduction
of Hemingway and, understandably, included in it the news
about his receiving the Dial Award: "A friend of mine and a
very delightful man, Ernest Hemingway, and his wife are
leaving for Paris . . . They will sail December 8th. . . . Hemingway is a young fellow of extraordinary talent and, I believe, will get somewhere." Anderson specified that Hemingway "is not like [Harold] Stearns," the former Associate
Editor of *The Dial* in its rowdy political phase, 1917-19, and
a man later portrayed in *The Sun Also Rises* as the bibulous
Harvey Stone, who sat all day in need of a shave, at the Rotonde with a pile of saucers before him. Sandwiching his
own news among other gossip, Anderson confided that "As
the big announcement of the 'DIAL of WARD' [*sic*] will
be made on the first, and as this letter will not reach you
before that time, I will betray no secret in telling you that it
is to be made to me."

Another letter of introduction went from Anderson to
Gertrude Stein, his fellow revolutionary as a leader of the

New Movement; Ernest Hemingway took the note with him across the Atlantic, and changed the wording of Anderson's letter in order to correct the Parisian address Anderson gave for the Hemingways. "I am writing this note," began Anderson in one of the more fateful introductions of the century, "to make you acquainted with my friend Ernest Hemingway, who with Mrs. Hemingway is going to Paris to live, and will ask him to drop it in the mails when he arrives there." Anderson formally described "Mr. Hemingway" as "an American writer instinctively in touch with everything worth-while going on here, and I know you will find Mr. and Mrs. Hemingway delightful people to know."

Such were Anderson's feelings — he was ever a man for emotional hyperbole — on December 3, 1921. He could not know, under the circumstances, that although his protegé greatly admired some of the master's tales and short stories — they were simply written; even, sometimes, beautifully written; and peopled with characters the writer knew and deeply cared for — the longer works, the novels, seemed by contrast strangely lacking in the fine qualities of the tales. In Hemingway's early talks with Gertrude Stein, he preferred not to praise Anderson's stories precisely because they were too good to make happy conversation with Miss Stein; mentioning them favorably was like mentioning one general favorably to another general. Nor could Hemingway give a poor opinion of Anderson's novels; that would have been bad, too, because it was criticizing one of her loyal supporters. The problem, which at bottom involved the three-sided rivalry of Sherwood Anderson, Gertrude Stein, and Ernest Hemingway, became even more acute after Hemingway read Anderson's *Dark Laughter,* a novel the youngest of the rivals thought so terribly bad, silly, and affected that in 1924 he could not keep from criticizing it in a parody, his first novel, *The Torrents of Spring.*

Gertrude Stein's Parisian salon was Hemingway's introduction to the world of the expatriate American writers and their little magazines. In her *Autobiography of Alice B. Toklas,* written after Hemingway and she had quarreled and therefore not always to be taken literally, Gertrude Stein remembered very well, a decade after the event, Hemingway's calling on her one afternoon with a letter of introduction from Sherwood Anderson. "He was an extraordinarily good-looking young man, twenty-three years old. . . . rather foreign looking, with passionately interested, rather than interesting eyes. He sat in front of Gertrude Stein and listened and looked." The two writers, disparate in so many ways except in their compulsive drives to dominate a milieu and a craft, talked away the afternoon and talked again, more and more, a great deal together. Hemingway had in those days and retained, in Gertrude Stein's eyes, a very good instinct for finding apartments in strange but pleasing localities and good *femmes de ménage* and good food. She visited, in the company of Alice B. Toklas, the Hemingways in their first apartment just off the Place du Tertre and spent the evening going over all the writing he had done, the novel that he had inevitably begun and the little poems afterwards printed by Robert McAlmon in the Contact Edition. Gertrude Stein rather liked the poems: they were direct and Kiplingesque (though the latter adjective seems a strange judgment). The novel she found wanting. "There is a great deal of description in this," she said, "and not particularly good description. Begin over and concentrate."

In *A Moveable Feast* (written, of course, long after their quarrel) Hemingway's version of the conversation has it that Miss Stein informed him she herself wanted to be published in the *Atlantic Monthly,* as indeed both writers would later be. She also told him that he was not a good enough writer to be published there or in *The Saturday Evening Post*; he might be some new sort of writer in his own way, but the first thing to remember was not to write stories that were *inaccrochable,* i. e., worse than unsalable, not even pawnable. Such a story was like a picture that a painter paints but that he cannot hang when he has a show and that nobody will buy because they cannot hang it either. As Hemingway recalled, Gertrude Stein's remark was made not about a novel but about "Up in Michigan," the only one of his stories she saw that she did not like. Disregarding Gertrude Stein's advice — sound enough, based as it was on the experience of having editors reject her own *inaccrochable* stories *(inaccrochable* in another sense) — proved Hemingway's undoing on at least one memorable occasion within the next few years.

In Miss Stein's book, she it was who encouraged Hemingway to give up journalism and to write creatively: "If you keep on doing newspaper work you will never see things, you will only see words and that will not do, that is of course if you intend to be a writer." To pursue the course she advised entailed making sacrifices. Hemingway announced, one visit, with great bitterness that Hadley was *enceinte* and that he was "too young to be a father." He made up his mind nevertheless to go to America, to work hard for a year and with what he would earn and what he had to settle down, "and he would give up newspaper work and make himself a writer."

But this is to anticipate events. In the spring of 1922 Hemingway was still feeling his way through his new environment, was learning the ways both of Paris and the expatriates among whom he had cast his lot in those months. He had to learn, for example, how to pick a safe path between Gertrude Stein, on the one hand, and Ezra Pound, on the other. They were engaged in one of those literary and personal feuds that enliven memoirs of the 1920's. In *A Moveable Feast* Hemingway says this particular feud started because Pound had sat down too quickly on a small, fragile, and doubtless, uncomfortable chair, which Hemingway thought it quite possible Gertrude Stein had given Pound on purpose — and which Pound had promptly either cracked or broken. In his hearsay gossip about the *casus belli,* Hemingway defended Pound against Miss Stein by pointing out that in her anger over his maladroitness, she never considered that her guest was a great poet and a gentle and generous man who could have accomodated himself in a chair of ordinary size. In Hemingway's postbellum view of the Pound-Stein feud, she rationalized the episode of the fragile chair as literary criticism in the seventh chapter of *The Autobiography of Alice B. Toklas,* and thus years later skillfully and maliciously disguised her real reasons for disliking Ezra Pound.

There Miss Stein told her side of the tale. Her first meeting with Pound was not altogether happy. Both writers liked to hold the floor, and as Pound was a dinner guest in Miss Stein's apartment, he took the floor for the evening and talked about Japanese prints. The hostess liked him but did not find him amusing. She said he was a village explainer, excellent if you were a village, but if you were not, not.

Pound's second visit was the disastrous, and final, one; he brought with him Scofield Thayer, fresh from the United States and eagerly inspecting European possibilities for his *Dial*. This time, said Gertrude Stein, it was worse than Japanese prints, it was much more violent. In his surprise at the violence, Pound fell out of Gertrude Stein's favorite little armchair, one that Alice Toklas, Miss Stein's lifelong companion, industriously tapestried with Picasso designs (in her own memoir, *What Is Remembered*, Miss Toklas refers to "a little footstool of petit point I had made after a design of Picasso"; the Germans apparently looted it in 1945); Gertrude Stein was furious. Finally Pound and Thayer left, nobody too well pleased. Miss Stein did not wish to see Pound again; he did not understand why, and when he met her one day near the Luxembourg Gardens, he told her, "But I do want to come to see you." "I am so sorry," answered Gertrude Stein, "but Miss Toklas has a bad tooth and besides we are busy picking wild flowers." All of which was literally true, added the memoirist of Alice Toklas's *Autobiography*, "like all of Gertrude Stein's literature, but it upset Ezra, and we never saw him again."

Scofield Thayer saw no such deviousness as Hemingway alleged, on the part of the authoress of *Tender Buttons*; he told Alyse Gregory that it was Miss Stein's favorite armchair Pound fell out of and said he left with Pound, appalled at Gertrude's violence. Thayer saw her as "five feet high and two feet wide," with "a dark brown face and small, wise old Jewess' eyes. She curls up in the corner of a divan and falls over like a doll in trying to receive editors. She possesses the homely finish of a brown buckram bean bag. In conversation she put it all over Ezra" — obviously she was determined not to be silenced by his eloquence a second time — "who got back by saying all sorts of things on the way home."

Despite the uneasiness of such encounters, the Hemingways might well be confident that they would be hospitably received in Paris, handed over as they had been to the expatriate circle of literati by the recipient of the first Dial Award. Within a few weeks, Ernest Hemingway had managed to bring off the difficult trick of becoming close friends with both Gertrude Stein and the man she was angry with — Ezra Pound. As for Pound, he could survive his snubbing in the Stein *ménage*. After all, he was the Paris Correspondent of *The Dial* and its paid if unofficial agent (from about April 1920 until about April 1923). One day Ezra and Mrs Pound sauntered into Shakespeare and Company, the Left-Bank bookshop of Sylvia Beach, and she introduced them to the young man mousing around the book shelves. Many years later Pound recalled Ernest Hemingway's reply to the introduction: "I have traveled four thousand miles to see *you*."

Pound had, in fact, introduced Scofield Thayer to Gertrude Stein when his Editor was en route to Vienna to live there awhile. Thayer was going to Vienna to seek help from a family acquaintance, Sigmund Freud. For three years, Pound and Thayer were in constant touch, by mail usually, more seldom by wire; as Thayer's headquarters remained in Vienna, while Pound's headquarters were in Paris (until 1924), their meetings were rare. The only mutual interest in their association was the business of *The Dial*. In almost complete contrast was the daily, informal companionship of Pound and Hemingway, and the two sets of relations, so very different, affected Hemingway's literary career at the very start of his years in Paris.

Scofield Thayer had corresponded with Ezra Pound for over a year and a half when the men met in Paris in July 1921. To his close friend Alyse Gregory, Thayer sent a letter on July 30, giving the details of that first meeting and already expressing what would become his invariable ambiguity toward Pound. Hemingway's first remarks about Pound in *A Moveable Feast* picture a great and lovable poet whose awkwardness was probably due to Gertrude Stein's malice. Thayer saw Pound first of all as "a queer duck": "One has observed him so awkward as unintentionally to knock over a waiter and then so self-conscious as to be unable to say he is sorry. But like most people he means well and unlike most other people he has a finer imagination." Indeed, at close quarters Pound, of whom Thayer had been seeing more rather than less, was "much more fair in his judgments than his correspondence and his books would warrant one to believe. For instance, he acknowledges that D. H. Lawrence is one of the two or three most important young men writing English today, and he confesses very sweetly to being so opposite in temperament and interest as to be unable to read the

Veil [?]." Thayer described a visit to Pound's flat on the Rue
des Saints-Peres: "When one arrives at his hotel on the street
of the Holy Fathers, one usually learns from the young lady
that Mr. Pound is *au bain*. But the young lady consents to
going upstairs to see Mr. Pound and to inquire if Mr. Pound
will see guests. Mr. Pound receives beaming and incisive,"
wearing "a pointed yellow beard and elliptical pince-nez
and an open Byronic collar and an omelette-yellow bathrobe.... When in the street Mr. Pound wears what a young
lady ..., having see us dining vis-à-vis chez Voisin, calls 'Mr.
Pound's artistic uniform.' "

At its best, the amiability of Pound and Thayer was
strained and ironic, and soon even this fragile cordiality was
shattered. If Pound was to Thayer's eye a queer duck in a
messy yellow bathrobe (when not wearing his artistic uniform), Thayer to Pound's eye was just another rich man to
be milked for the sake of artists and art. Their relation met
its fatal test during the very months in which Hemingway
was getting to know Paris and meeting the people who became his acquaintances and enemies and advisors. Just when
Pound was making friends with Hemingway, he was serving
as the mentor of an older friend, T. S. Eliot, during the composition and revision of *The Waste Land*. By January 30,
1922, Eliot was able to offer the poem to Thayer for publication exclusively in *The Dial*; on January 29, Thayer accepted
it, sight unseen, and offered to pay $150, a round sum, for
a poem that had been described to him as of 450 lines, about
eleven pages of printed matter in *The Dial*. Eliot did not
agree to those terms and wired instead that he could not
accept less than 856 pounds. The Editor responded urbanely,
presuming in his answering letter that there must have been
some error on the part of the telegraph service; nevertheless
he told Eliot that, in the meantime, he had to notify *The
Dial* "that we are apparently not to receive the poem." Pound
tried his best to come to Eliot's aid. On February 18, he was
enthusiastically recommending his friend's work to Thayer:
it was important, almost enough to make everyone else shut
up shop. The "almost" was an important qualification, for
in those weeks Pound sent an "Eighth Canto" to Watson, at
the *Dial* offices in New York, and also wrote Watson and
Seldes that Eliot had composed an important sequence of

poems. On March 9, Thayer cabled his two colleagues the distressing news that Eliot had withdrawn *The Waste Land* from consideration by *The Dial*; and it was not until July of 1922 that Watson, then in London during a summer trip to Europe, was able to patch things together and secure *The Waste Land* for his magazine.

Eventually, then, *The Waste Land* was published in *The Dial* for November 1922; but Eliot's success did not aid Pound's other friend, Ernest Hemingway. To the contrary, Hemingway's first attempt to publish his work in *The Dial* could hardly have been more badly timed. Perhaps he was hopeful of succeeding with *The Dial* because of his connections: with Sherwood Anderson, not only recipient of the first Dial Award but apparently one of the mainstays of the magazine; and with Ezra Pound, Paris Correspondent and paid agent of *The Dial* and as important a contributor as Anderson. And at the start of his friendship with Pound, Hemingway was probably not aware that by taking sides with Eliot about *The Waste Land,* Pound had drawn down upon himself the wrath of the Editor of *The Dial*. Doubtless Thayer was irritated also by the fussy, proprietary manner of Pound, who did tend, rather, to act as though he not only had founded but owned the New Movement lock, stock, and barrel, and in the long run the two men — so different in their selfless, absolute dedication to art — were bound to collide. At the beginning of his career, unfortunately, Hemingway was a sacrifice to a literary feud.

Most probably it was in February 1922 that Ezra Pound sent Scofield Thayer a group of poems by Hemingway. That procedure was the custom for Pound to follow with regard to *The Dial,* an essential aspect of the job for which the magazine paid him $750 a year: he was a literary scout and contact man. Hemingway recalls this kind of service, in which Pound was the literary entrepreneur, in much less formal terms, however, in the story "Ezra Pound and His Bel Esprit," in *A Moveable Feast* and merely remarks that Ezra Pound was always a good friend to him and to others and was always helpful to people in their Paris group. And again, with greater detail and in the same spirit, Hemingway says that Pound was the most generous writer he ever knew — a remarkable tribute and one not the less remarkable for its having been said at the end of Hemingway's long career as a writer. Pound was, moreover, the most disinterested of literary men, that is to say, he did not charge an agent's fee for helping to sell a manuscript, and his services performed for the writers he befriended were altruistic. As Hemingway saw Pound in the early 1920's, the older man helped poets, painters, prose writers whom he believed in; these artists did not have to be in difficulties for Pound to lend a helping hand, he helped the younger artists simply because he believed in them. Pound's concern for his acquaintances was perhaps most famously expressed in his relation to T. S. Eliot, who, Pound told Hemingway, had to work bad hours in a bank in London and thus lacked sufficient leisure to function adequately as a poet.

Hemingway became a member of the Bel Esprit group, a sort of corporation Pound formed to support a specified artist or writer; and the assertion accords with Pound's correspondence with Thayer about Eliot and *The Waste Land*. In a letter dated March 9-10, 1922, Pound protested to Thayer that Eliot should have had the first Dial Award, not Sherwood Anderson; Eliot's breakdown would respond to rest; perhaps it would be preferable to chuck *The Dial* and pension him off, to get him out of his bank. The outcome of Pound's urging and badgering in March 1922 was his formation of Bel Esprit, along with, according to Hemingway, Natalie Barney, a rich American woman who patronized the arts; she was the intimate friend of Pound's great admiration, the recently deceased Rémy de Gourmont, and a pillar of the upper storeys of Parisian bohemian-expatriate society.

Pound's proposal for Bel Esprit at length appeared, and not by accident, in *The Dial* for November 1922 in company with *The Waste Land*. A part of the agreement, finally reached with Thayer and Watson, to publish the poem in *The Dial* was that Eliot would receive the Dial Award for 1922. It was duly announced as his in the issue for January 1923. The crack-up of Bel Esprit, thought Hemingway, thus had a connection with the American publication of *The Waste Land*, which gained for "Major" Eliot the Dial Award, the military title of "Major" being Hemingway's epithet for Eliot, coined through a pretended confusion of Eliot with Major C. H. Douglas, the founder of Social-Credit economics and a friend as greatly admired by Pound as was Eliot. As Hemingway explained the sequence of cause and effect in this portion of Eliot's advancing renown, not long after the announcement of the Dial Award to Eliot, a lady of title (actually Viscountess Rothermere) backed for Eliot a new review, *The Criterion,* and Pound and his friends no longer had to worry about Eliot. Hemingway's anecdote is an interesting bit of apocrypha: for a year and more, in 1921-22, Eliot and Scofield Thayer had discussed the publication of a British version of *The Dial,* with Eliot as its editor; but because of the trouble over publishing *The Waste Land,* and also because of Lady Rothermere's reluctance to advance the large sums needed to establish another *Dial,* Eliot's quarterly, *The Criterion,* was started in October 1922 and published his *Waste Land,* in its first number, at the same time *The Dial* published the poem in New York.

In the very weeks in which Pound was fighting for the publication of *The Waste Land* in *The Dial,* he was, equally pugnaciously, taking boxing lessons from the young writer whose poems he sent to Thayer in Vienna. The lessons had been requested by Pound, and the sparring took place in his studio. Wyndham Lewis dropped in late one afternoon, and out of consideration for Pound, who had not been boxing very long, Hemingway tried to make him look as good as possible, despite the difficulty of this good deed. Pound knew how to fence, but he was unteachable as a boxer. The agile instructor tried to teach his awkward pupil just the basic moves — how to make the left hand into the boxing hand, how to move the left foot forward always, how to bring up the right foot parallel with the left. But Pound never learned to throw a left hook, and this particular session in the studio ended without any improvement in his shortening his right hook.

The observer at these exercises, Wyndham Lewis, was a master at intellectual feinting and jabbing and may have taught Ernest Hemingway a thing or two about literary infighting a few years later. The first round was undeniably Lewis's; his critique of Hemingway, "Ernest Hemingway (the 'Dumb Ox')," came out in 1934 at a time when the ox's reputation was at its height, when, at least in America, it seemed positively un-American to decry Hemingway's talent.

Yet decry it Wyndham Lewis did. Hemingway's work possessed, wrote Lewis, "a penetrating quality, like an animal
speaking," and if the critic expressed any admiration for
Hemingway's stories, he did so in a maddeningly qualified
fashion: "The expression of the soul of the dumb ox would
have a penetrating beauty of its own, if it were uttered with
genius — with bovine genius (and in the case of Hemingway
that is what has happened): just as much as would the folk-
song of the baboon, or the 'Praying Mantis.' " And Lewis
concluded that if one took Hemingway's art to be the typical
art of a civilization — "and there is no serious writer who
stands higher in Anglo-Saxony today than does Ernest Hemingway — then we are by the same token saying something
very definite about civilization."

Perhaps by default (Wyndham Lewis died in 1957), the
second round, in 1960, went to Hemingway — or, to change the
metaphor, the dumb ox gored his tormenting matador and
drew blood. On first acquaintance, Hemingway saw Lewis
as a little frog in the big puddle of Paris, just another character
in the fancy dress of the Quarter, decked out like one of the
chorus in *La Bohème*. He was a man who did not show evil
but merely looked ineffably nasty, the nastiest man Ernest
Hemingway had seen in all his twenty-three years, a man, to
sum up, with the eyes of an unsuccessful rapist. Gertrude
Stein, noted Hemingway, called Wyndham Lewis the Measuring Worm on account of his habit, when in a Parisian
gallery, of looking at a picture, taking a pencil out of his
pocket, and measuring it on the pencil with his thumb. Then,
she related accusingly, Lewis would return to London, try
his best to imitate the technique of the picture he had admired
and analyzed — but invariably to no effect. He had missed
what the original was all about. There is just a single nag-
ging question in the back of one's mind about this otherwise
entertaining blackguarding of Wyndham Lewis, not an attractive man but to other tastes an interesting artist: if, by
Ernest Hemingway's own assurances, the reader should not believe Gertrude Stein speaking about Ezra Pound, then why
should one believe her gossip about Wyndham Lewis?

Those afternoons spent unsuccessfully sweating over
Pound's left hook thus offered their less engaging hours.
And on another level they failed, too. If Pound's boxing

was maladroit, so for the *The Dial* was Hemingway's poetry; Scofield Thayer read Hemingway's poems and rejected them as unsuitable. In a long letter to Pound, dated March 5, 1922, Thayer devoted a paragraph to his Paris correspondent's latest enthusiasm: "I was interested to see the poems by Ernest Hemingway. I am however of the opinion that the The Dial has enough young blood already to make it decidedly rough reading. I have therefore been unable to accept even those examples of Mr. Hemingway's art which you as always so perceptively point out to be the better ones." Charles Fenton says that Pound sent six of Hemingway's poems to Thayer, but Thayer's letter to Pound does not specify the number of poems Hemingway submitted to *The Dial*. Thayer merely added to Pound that he had sent "the things" directly back to the author. It may have been in an accompanying letter — of which no record exists in the *Dial* files — that the Editor of *The Dial* advised Hemingway to return to reporting, where his future as a writer lay. Whatever the case, on March 9, 1922, Hemingway wrote to Sherwood Anderson in words that suggest a strong reaction to Thayer's rejection of the group of poems submitted to *The Dial*. He said that "this goddam newspaper stuff is gradually ruining me" and described his plans to "cut it all loose pretty soon and work for about three months." Oftentimes being turned down acts not as a discouragement but as a spur to gallop faster toward the goal and to win the prize, and it may well be that Hemingway's rejection by *The Dial* inspired him all the more determinedly to forsake journalism for his more serious vocation as a writer of stories and novels.

CHAPTER 2

"THE scum of Greenwich Village, New York, has been skimmed off and deposited in large ladlesful on that section of Paris adjacent to the Café Rotonde. New scum, of course, has risen to take the place of the old, but the oldest scum, the thickest scum and the scummiest scum has come across the ocean, somehow, and with its afternoon and evening levees has made the Rotonde the leading Latin Quarter show place for tourists in search of atmosphere," Hemingway wrote, in the weekly magazine of the *Toronto Star* for March 25, 1922. After a few weeks of Paris, he had become if not disillusioned at any rate superior to those whom he described in the title of his article as "American Bohemians in Paris." They were, he told his Canadian readers, "a strange-acting and strange-looking breed that crowd the tables of the Café Rotonde. They have all striven so hard for a careless individuality of clothing that they have a sort of uniformity of eccentricity," and a first look into the smoky, high-ceilinged, table-crammed interior of the Rotonde gave him the same feeling that hit him as he might step "into the bird house at the zoo." A tremendous, raucous, many-pitched squawking resounded; waiters flew about through the smoke like so many black-and-white magpies; the incessant jumbled movement of people confused the perception that tried to pick out an individual at one of the full, crowded tables or at an entrance way. A little was enough, for the men and women who crowded together around the tables of the Café Rotonde did something very definite to "that premier seat of the emotions, the stomach." Hemingway contrasted Charles Baudelaire favorably to any one of the gang that congregated at the corner of the Boulevard Montparnasse and the Boulevard Raspail; because they put in a full day at the Rotonde, they had no time to work at anything else. (However, it was not Baudelaire who, according to Hemingway, "led a purple lobster on a leash through the same old Latin Quarter" but Gérard de Nerval, much more at home with the predecessors of the gang at the Rotonde than was Baudelaire.)

Yet these were the readers, the contributors, the editors and, in a few cases, the backers of the little literary journals and the little literary presses that published the experimental writing to which Hemingway, for all his hard work as a reporter for the *Toronto Star,* dedicated himself. His earliest writing that was creative saw the light in little magazines and small editions of the presses founded to publish work unacceptable to the established magazines and publishers. Several of those who frequented the Rotonde and the Café du Dôme were soon to be important to Hemingway in his attempt to achieve recognition for his writing: Ezra Pound, Ford Madox Ford, William Bird, and Robert McAlmon among others. His contempt for the gang at the Rotonde was assumed in part; there is a strong probability that the tone — mingled of condescension, cynicism, and shocked prudery toward the Bohemians who rebelled against the gospel of work — that dominates Hemingway's piece in the *Star*'s weekly magazine was designed to please the more easily shockable of his Toronto readers.

A very different picture of the same scene is painted by Arthur Moss in *The Double-Dealer* for May 1922; this little magazine of the arts — it announced itself as "A National Magazine from the South" — was published from New Orleans, and New Orleans has always been notoriously ad-

dicted to having a good time. Moss's letter about Paris thus
fell into friendly hands. "One cannot sit in the Café de la
Rotonde five minutes," Moss told his New Orleans correspondents, "without being hailed by Americans of all varieties
of the seven arts. Among the expatriates are Harold Stearns,
editor of 'Civilization in the United States'; the sculptors,
Paul Manship and Jo Davidson; Man Ray, whom the Zarai-
stas [sic] have named the American Dada; Sinclair Lewis,
who for some curious and unexplained reason seems to prefer
Boulevard Montparnasse to Main Street; Hiram K. Moder-
well, author of 'The Theater of Today,' . . . Joseph Kling,
editor of *Pagan*, arrived recently." To Moss the work of the
American artists at the Salon des Indépendants — he named
Paul Burlin, Man Ray, Julian Levi, Waldo Peirce, Abel
Warshawsky, Janet Scudder, and Morgan Russell — rivaled
that of the Europeans (except for the sculpture of Jacques
Lipchitz and the paintings of Matisse, Picasso, Gleizes, Lhote,
"and a few others"). The French men of letters were going
in heavily for American works; *Main Street* was being translated, and the critics seemed particularly interested in Waldo
Frank, Carl Sandburg, Sherwood Anderson, and the other
writers "who present material so thoroughly local as to be
unmistakably American from a French viewpoint." And, as
an item of special significance to New Orleans, Moss pointed
out that the famous "Groupe des Six" were "greatly influenced by American 'blues,' which they insist on classifying
and I think rightly, as American folk-music."

Moss's more optimistic and less sensational view of go-
ings on around Paris appeared in *The Double-Dealer* a few
pages to the rear of Ernest Hemingway's contribution, a
brief fable of two pages entitled "A Divine Gesture" — outside his reportage, his first publication as a professional writer.
The Double-Dealer accepted "A Divine Gesture" precisely
because it showed promise rather than achievement; that
is to say, because of Hemingway's irony and black humor in
portraying a dictatorial, indifferent Deity and His angels and
a trivial, unimportant humankind.

If only by indirection, Hemingway's fable protested such
a state of affairs; and like his story, *The Double-Dealer*, too,
protested. It indeed had been founded in January 1921 to
protest the *status quo* in the Deep South, and in an editorial

in its issue for April 1921 said that, with all due modesty, it wished to be known "as the rebuilder, the driver of the first pile into the mud of this artistic stagnation which has been our portion since the Civil War. The magazine is, beyond this, a movement, a protest, arising up against the intellectual tyranny of New York, New England, and the Middle West." Julius Friend and Basil Thompson were the editors, and they were assisted by Albert Goldstein and John McClure as associate editors. The entire roster of the staff suggested youth; the only nationally known name on the masthead was that of the Chicago Correspondent, Vincent Starrett. What more fitting place for one in rebellion to be published?

Hemingway's appearance as a serious creative writer nevertheless is, on the surface of the event, a strange opposition to his life as a roving foreign correspondent to perhaps the most important Canadian newspaper. His milieu at the time was international, controlled by the sense of fact and observation, oriented toward the Protestant middle-class readership of a daily newspaper in a large North American city. Yet the first fruit of Hemingway's attempt to quit journalism appeared in a journal strenuously advocating the revival of a regional literature in the Catholic Deep South of New Orleans. The opposition of the two milieux is typified in the contrasting reports, by Hemingway and Arthur Moss, of the habitués of the Café de la Rotonde in the spring of 1922. One story relishes the depravity of the gang — that aimless, rootless, worthless gang! — congregating on the street corners and perching in the cafés of the Latin Quarter; the other story understands that for the first time (except for Poe's work) the literature and art and music being produced by Americans were inspiring many French writers, artists, composers.

Why then, if his antipathy was real, was Hemingway becoming dissatisfied with journalism and attempting to enroll in the lists of the contributors to the literary journals of the New Movement? He must have been aware that he might look forward to a distinguished future as a foreign correspondent or, if he so desired, as a columnist or editorial writer. Perhaps to a degree Gertrude Stein did influence him, in the course of 1922-23, to forego newspaper work for more serious writing. More likely he would have done so anyway. His new life in Paris, however, provided Hemingway with the company and the examples he needed to turn him in the direction of the road he took.

And he himself has provided the most convincing answer to the query. In his latter years, in "A Situation Report," published in *Look* for September 4, 1956, Ernest Hemingway wrote one of those curious and characteristic betwixt-and-between pieces in which he veered between the popular descriptive articles he turned out in the early 1920's for the Toronto *Star Weekly* and the more inward self-analysis of the notable passages in *Green Hills of Africa*. In the latter vein, the lengthy epigraph of the article in *Look* was a quotation from Cyril Connolly's *The Unquiet Grave*, a kind of *journal intime* almost totally dissimilar from most of "A Situation Report," which recounted a famous writer's night out surrounded by an admiring "honor guard" of navy CPO's drinking at the Floridita bar in Havana. Taking Connolly's epigraph as his text, Hemingway told the readers of *Look* that here was a book which, "no matter how many readers it will ever have, will never have enough." Most revealingly, Hemingway specified his approval of the epigraph itself, a very personal assessment of a dedicated writer's *raison d'être*, in which Connolly declared that the more books we read, "the sooner we perceive that the true function of a writer is to produce a masterpiece and that no other task is of any consequence. Obvious though this should be, how few writers will admit it, or having made the admission, will be prepared to lay aside the piece of iridescent mediocrity on which they have embarked! Writers always hope that their next book is going to be their best, for they will not acknowledge that it is their present way of life which prevents them ever creating anything different or better." And Connolly asserted that all excursions into journalism, broadcasting, propaganda, and writing for the films, "however grandiose, are doomed to disappointment. To put of our best into these forms is another folly, since thereby we condemn good ideas, as well as bad, to oblivion. It is in the nature of such work not to last, so it should never be undertaken."

Hemingway commented that rereading that passage "and having interrupted a book that you loved and believed in on the eight hundred and fiftieth manuscript page, to work four months on the script and photography" of *The Old Man and the Sea,* "another book that you believed in and loved, you know now that now you will never again interrupt the work that you were born and trained to do until you die. Since in almost any week you can read the obituaries of good dead friends, this is not much of a promise. But it is one that you can keep." In the light of this commitment, it is clear that for Hemingway publication of his early writing in the little magazines, as well as the effort to become an artist as a writer, was not just a matter of second best. He went hungry until he could impose his vision upon the millions of readers who were not even aware they were awaiting that astonishing insight.

Y. K. Smith told Charles Fenton that Hemingway "hated the idea of a nine to five job . . . . He wanted his freedom. He had no illusions about journalism, but he'd concluded that it was at least better than anything else he'd seen." Hemingway's reporting, conscientious, even brilliant at its best, offered an insufficient challenge, it was work that he could do well with half his mind, and that not the better half. The life of art was thus not to remain for Hemingway a mere *violon d'Ingres,* an avocation for weekends or for weeks between assignments as a reporter. In Chicago in 1920 Hemingway had, without success, tried his luck with magazines ranging from *Argosy* to *Vanity Fair,* to which last he sent out satirical rewrites of world news. During those months in Chicago in the fall and early winter of 1920 when Hemingway made friends with Sherwood Anderson, he typed away the evenings in his room in Y. K. Smith's apartment on the near North Side, "in a mood of almost buckshot literary endeavor," as Charles Fenton has put it. Besides poetry and topical satire and stories for a men's pulp magazine, Hemingway also wrote the prose fable that *The Double-Dealer* printed.

That Hemingway had ever met any of the staff of *The Double-Dealer* is doubtful, and the strong likelihood is that he never submitted either "A Divine Gesture" or his other contribution, a quatrain entitled "Ultimately," to the editors. Rather it was Sherwood Anderson who did so. Agreeing with Hemingway himself, Anderson never claimed to have

influenced Hemingway's work as a whole. He did say it was
"through my efforts" that Hemingway "first got published."
And in his posthumously published memoirs of 1942, Anderson wrote that anyway it was sure "that if others said I had
shown Hemingway the way, I myself had never said so. I
thought . . . that he had his own gift, which had nothing to do
with me." Anderson was spending the winter and spring
of 1922 down in New Orleans, and nothing was more natural
than that he should meet Julius Friend, James Feibleman,
Basil Thompson, and others among the group bringing out
The Double-Dealer. Like Anderson, these young people were
in search of identity, personal and national but also regional.
Their attraction was mutual. Anderson for them and for
Hemingway was a catalyzing agent.

Anderson's presence both in Hemingway's early professional career and among the younger writers and artists of
New Orleans was, of course, important and inspiring; he
seems to have been wholeheartedly accepted in New Orleans,
however ironically and partially Hemingway accepted him.
That is to say, Anderson's primitivist and regional qualities
as a novelist answered the needs of Hemingway and the young
men and women of *The Double-Dealer*; but soon Hemingway violently rejected altogether the regionalism of Anderson's fiction and with equal violence rejected Anderson's
aesthetic primitivism, what, with pride, Anderson termed his
"crudity." The significance of Sherwood Anderson as a god
to be worshipped in the little magazines of the New Movement by his votaries or alternatively to be cast down and
shattered by his erstwhile disciple is explicable in terms of the
conflicting factions within the New Movement. To simplify,
these were the nativists, as Anderson always was, and the
internationalists, as T. S. Eliot was (or as, in Marxist politico-
aesthetic terms, Max Eastman and John Reed were back
then). To the nativists, the subject was a region — a place
and its traditions. To the internationalists, technique was
the paramount concern, technique as expression of the self.
One kind of writer sought to fit himself into the region. The
other kind of writer used a scene, a place, to express himself
through, as an image of his inner vision. Occasionally a
writer like Paul Rosenfeld mediated between the two fac-

tions and espousing dogmas held by one camp or the other, evolved a personal eclecticism.

Hemingway began his career as a nativist, a writer whose Nick Adams stories were nothing if not regional in inspiration; yet at the same time he wrote the vignettes of *in our time* — etching scenes as disparate as a Spanish bullfight, soldiers fighting in a garden, the flight of refugees in the Greco-Turkist War — that eschew anything regional and that, for all the geographical and social disparity, express an inner vision of violence and destruction. The latter vein of writing rapidly dominated Hemingway's stories and novels and memoirs; Hemingway forsook his regions of northern Michigan and Chicago, and his stories and novels, as known to most readers, are as expatriate and international in setting as are those of Henry James and Edith Wharton. Pulled away by the force of his obsession with finding the technique best suited to express his private vision, Hemingway gravitated from Anderson as a model and never again published in a regional little magazine after his two appearances in *The Double-Dealer*; and even in his first publication his writing was opposed to the specifically regional protest of *The Double-Dealer*. "A Divine Gesture" and "Ultimately" are, like much that appeared in the magazine, antibourgeois and intended to convey their below-the-surface irony through the device of shock-by-realism; but regional pieces they are not. The thrust of Hemingway's talent was consistently toward the ideal of such a literary journal as *The Transatlantic Review*, toward the international point of view, and toward the assimilation by that point of view of qualities, subjects, style, and settings specifically American.

In this context, Sherwood Anderson's relation to *The Double-Dealer* is important to examine in some detail; doing so shows his limitation as model and helper to Hemingway and the incongruity of Hemingway as his protegé. That Anderson was an inspiration for *The Double-Dealer* Hart Crane first made clear in its issue for July 1921. The time had already arrived, said Crane, when Anderson was beginning to be recognized as among "the first few recorders of the life of a people coming to some state of self-consciousness." Without sentimentality, not pretending to offer solutions, with a humanity and simplicity baffling in depth and

suggestiveness, his steady, deliberate growth was proving the
promise of finer work. Anderson's first appearance in *The
Double-Dealer,* in February 1922, was in accord with Crane's
image of him. With a set of gnomic sayings, "A New Testament," he expressed his status as Messiah of the New Movement through such prophetic utterances as "It is not true that
God created the world in six days, or rather perhaps he did —
a fact that would account for the corruption of the world.
Worlds should be created as gestures of gods." A curious
compound of La Rochefoucould's maxims, Bronson Alcott's
Orphic sayings, and Nietzschean declamation, Anderson's
utterance might well have been appropriated for the epigraph to Hemingway's fable in the May 1922 *Double-Dealer.*
The next month, March 1922, a *Double-Dealer* editorial,
"Back to Chaos," asked with regard to Sherwood Anderson:
"What is the meaning of all this eloquence about chaos,
crudity, and dancing stars? The idea is not new, an old
tattered thing if you will, but stale, tattered, old, as it is, it
remains the vitalest thing in the development of an emerging
people." Anderson had stated the idea: "crudity is an inevi-
table quality in the production of a really significant present-
day American literature." Only by going back to the elemental, "or rather by beginning with the elemental, the
simple, the real, the unsubtle, the crude" would the voice of
America ever be heard or worth the hearing.

In that issue of the magazine, Anderson returned the
editorial compliment in a rhapsodic paean to "New Orleans,
The Double Dealer, and the Modern Movement," in which
he proclaimed himself "an American and one of the Mod-
erns" and then identified the Modern Movement with the
life expressive of the Vieux Carré in New Orleans, a life he
thought America wanted and needed, "something that made
its people like one another, that led to constant outbursts
of the spirit of play, that kept them from being too con-
foundedly serious about death and the ballot and reform and
other less important things." Anderson advocated the
"quieter, more leisurely, and altogether charming way of
life" Americans might begin to live, not in Europe (a jab
at the expatriates) but in America. After all, when it came
to the Arts, it was probably true that there was more vitality
"to the Modern Art Movement, as expressed in America in

sculpture, painting and writing, than in any of the older cultural centers of Europe." In an ecstasy of the regional afflatus, Anderson saw that perhaps the South had only been "waiting for the Modern Spirit to assert itself to come into its own" and that it was coming into its own " a little through such efforts as the publication of *The Double Dealer*, a magazine devoted to the arts, in New Orleans." The Modern Spirit meant nothing to him if it did not mean putting the joy of living "above the much less subtle and I think altogether stupid joy of growth and achievement." New Orleans seemed on the way to becoming the Florence of a Southern Renaissance.

Two months after that manifesto, there came without warning the anticlimactic announcement in the May 1922 *Double-Dealer* that "having completed his pilgrimage to New Orleans," Sherwood Anderson had "returned to Chicago to write copy for an important advertising campaign. We look for his return next winter." So New Orleans was forsaken for the time being, while Sherwood Anderson indulged Chicago's altogether stupid joy of growth and achievement, in an important advertising campaign. It was as an advertising man that Anderson had come to know Hemingway, when he was rooming at the apartment Y. K. Smith, of the Critchfield advertising firm, was subletting from the wealthy Chicago writer and patron, Mary Aldis; and it was as an advertising man of sorts that Anderson had puffed the advantages of New Orleans in *The Double-Dealer*. The profundity of his attachment to the Vieux Carré is gauged by the length of his stay, about three months. "New Orleans, the Double Dealer, and the Modern Movement in America" was by intention an assertion of the virtue of a region and its possibilities for the arts and literature as against the demands of, say, New York and Paris. But Anderson's overblown praise degenerated into mere provincialism, the validity of which could not withstand a dispassionate inspection. Add to it a crude and undigested element of rhetorical inflation and a mistrust of the conscious and craftsmanly creation of a story, and one understands why Ernest Hemingway wrote *The Torrents of Spring* as a corrective. In sum, Sherwood Anderson's manifesto was a piece of advertising, no more.

Despite his desertion of the Vieux Carré, the May issue

of *The Double-Dealer* is a lively and interesting one, containing as it did Edmund Wilson's ballad "Quintilian,"
Djuna Barnes's story "Vagaries Malicieux," Hart Crane's
translation of Jules Laforgue's "Locutions des Pierrots," and
— to show that the South did indeed assert the Modern Spirit
as much as Chicago or Paris — two poems by young Southern-
ers, Allen Tate's "Euthanasia," and William Alexander Per-
cy's "Beth Marie." In their company Ernest Hemingway
made his debut as a man of letters — auspicious company if
not an auspicious debut — with his brief fable in prose, "A
Divine Gesture."

"A Divine Gesture" opens as the Great Lord God strides
from his house into the garden, "for in the garden he found
the deep peace of Rome." Bathtubs stand around in heavy
earnestness. Boot jacks litter the garden. A thousand broken
flower pots are piled into one corner. God asks for Adam
and there is silence. Pulling at his beard and looking remarkably like Tolstoi, God asks for Eve. The largest and weakest
of the bathtubs answers that she is away and that "no man can
prophecy the hour of her returning. But I should say she
should return around four o'clock." Whereupon the angel
Gabriel lets all the water out of that bathtub, to teach him a
"valuable lesson." The boot jacks begin curling and uncurl-
ing in an alarming manner. God shouts to them to "Stop it!"
They are still momentarily but are soon squirming and chanting at the top of their voices, "We mustn't squirm today! Ha
Ya Ta Did Eeyay!" God stops the racket and tells the boot
jacks that He is busier than ever. They nevertheless again begin chanting and squirming. God strides away in disgust, making "a divine gesture" to the angel Gabriel, who follows Him
quietly out of the garden. "No peace," says the Great Lord
God as the pair stride rapidly up the long stairs, "no peace
anywhere. I'm so busy, and there is only twenty-four hours
in a day." Gabriel corrects God's grammar: "Are twenty-four
hours you perhaps mean, Sire." But God answers, "Is twenty-
four hours, I mean." And the angel Gabriel smiles uncer-
tainly and follows God up the long stairs, thinking of his
wife and children. Resting for a little while in their climb-
ing, far below them they can hear the sound of the boot jacks
squirming and chanting. "What is that sound?" asks God,
for "like many other leaders he was very deaf at times." "Your

faithful boot jacks, Sire," answers Gabriel quietly, but very distinctly. "Ah, yes," God muses happily, "my faithful boot jacks."

Years later, in *The New Yorker*, James Thurber wrote similar seriocomic fables, using in much the same way a vocabulary that wavered between the romantic and the everyday. The genre of the fable had an enduring attraction for Hemingway; he returned to it in 1951, when in the March issue of *Holiday*, the glossy Curtis magazine of travel and entertainment, he published two fables, "The Good Lion" and "The Faithful Bull." In so doing, he was not imitating Thurber's popular fables of the 1940's but was returning all the way back to his beginnings and "A Divine Gesture."

For the background of "A Divine Gesture" lies in Hemingway's months of journalistic hack work in Chicago in 1920-21. There he accumulated ample matter for satirical reflection. Turning out fifty to sixty pages a month on such topics as "What Is Idealism?" for Harrison Parker's *Co-operative Commonwealth* furnished him with material for social satire contrasting the easy idealism of the middle class with the state of things as they are.

The form of his little fable is, however, partly at odds with its social comment in the tradition of American naturalism. In one sense that form is weak and rather obviously derivative: "A Divine Gesture" seems in keeping with the illustrated covers *The Double-Dealer* then printed, Olive Leonhardt's pseudo-Beardsley pictures of Pierrots and Columbines at, presumably, some Mardi-Gras fête. The fanciful setting, the symbolism of the story, the occasionally portentous diction — appropriate to *The Yellow Book* or *The Savoy* — are derivative and inadequately realized. The symbolist element, moreover, does not accord with the naturalist impulse driving the fable to its conclusion.

In another sense, the form of "A Divine Gesture" is its only truly distinctive and most personal element, stronger than its satirical social comment. This positive aspect of the fable is Hemingway's literary burlesque of other fables. He reduces the grand and serious to the low and trivial: the realistic chanting of the boot jacks instead of the psalms of the saints, the use of the bathtub as symbol of the spokesman of God's creatures, the transformation of God into a harried tycoon or prime minister and of Gabriel into a yes-man afraid for his family and his job. This element in Hemingway's fable distinguished it from anything Sherwood Anderson was capable of creating: an acute, cruel, comic wit more sophisticated, complex, and probing than mere mimicry.

"A Divine Gesture" is a burlesque of a kind of fable that was still popular in the early 1920's, that Oscar Wilde had written in the 1880's, and that Ronald Firbank had experimented with at the very start of his career in the Edwardian decade. Charles Fenton has described "A Divine Gesture" as being in the manner of Anatole France or Ben Hecht. One hardly needs to go afield to French literature for a model, or, rather, one hardly need stop at French literature; since the 1890's the symbolist fable had been a vehicle used with distinction by Hugo von Hofmannsthal, the Austrian poet and dramatist, as well as the Belgian Maurice Maeterlinck. As for Hecht, Hemingway may have known of him as a newspaperman in Chicago, perhaps also as an early contributor to Margaret Anderson's *Little Review* before it moved from Chicago to Greenwich Village; but Hecht's work was not necessary as a model.

"A Divine Gesture" echoed writing of the times as easily available and as popular as Hecht's. At one level it recalls the realistic impulse in style and intention of George Ade's fables. Like Hecht and Hemingway, Ade had started in Chicago as a reporter; in 1899 he collected his satirical pieces as *Fables in Slang*. Ade's realistic devices of setting the old form of the fable in the Midwest, usually the urban Midwest, and of telling the events of the fables in the slang then current proved a hit; his stories enjoyed a vogue both widespread and long-lived. As late as 1920, a brief review in *The Dial* for May said approvingly that in his new book of *Hand-Made Fables*, Ade demonstrated once more the capacities of American slang vernacular for clearness, force and " (yes!) elegance that quite escape the base-ball reporter." At another level, "A Divine Gesture" recalls the vague, grandiose style of Kahlil Gibran, the expatriate Lebanese seer and artist, whose symbolist prose-poetry had affinities in style and imagery with the symbolist fable. Gibran was taken seriously by certain of the vanguard. In July 1920 *The Dial* printed "Seven Sayings" of his that positively invited parody, the first of which confusingly reads, "I said to Life, 'I would hear Death speak,' and Life raised her voice a little higher and said, 'You hear it now.' "

What is perhaps not so apparent is that "A Divine Gesture" besides generally burlesquing a decadent style and form is specifically a parody of Sherwood Anderson's prose-poems, of which *The Double-Dealer*'s "A New Testament" is representative. These are best read in his volume of 1927, which brought together fifty-seven of his prose-poems and dialogues, those already in print and those not yet made public. Dedicated to Horace Liveright, the book was published by Boni and Liveright in a limited edition of 265 copies. Several of the prose-poems were acknowledged as having been reprinted from Anderson's *The Triumph of the Egg*, his successful volume of 1921, but the Zarathrustran pronouncement entitled "A New Testament" in *The Double-Dealer* was reprinted, without acknowledgement to the magazine, as "A Thinker," and its title was transferred to the collection as a whole. There is of course no telling whether Hemingway had read *The Triumph of the Egg* and "A New Testament," although it is a safe assumption he had; and there is no telling how many of Anderson's oracular prose-poems the author had read to Hemingway and his friends in Chicago in 1921, although it is surely safe to assume that Hemingway must have become familiar with Anderson's style at this time. Y. K. Smith told Charles Fenton that one evening in the Smith apartment, after Anderson had left, taking with him the story he had just read aloud, Hemingway remarked, "You couldn't let a sentence like that go."

In "A Divine Gesture," Hemingway was *not* letting some of Anderson's sentences go. At a fairly simple level, he was imitating such Andersonian verbalizings as "A Thinker": "Worlds should be created as gestures of gods." There are other verbal reminiscences, as from "The Man with a Trumpet": ". . . I might have plunged through walls . . . gone outward to the doorstep of the house of God, gone to God's throne room with their hands in mine." At a more complex level, "A Divine Gesture" echoes the declamatory repetitions and the simple parallel constructions of such a piece as "The Dumb Man": "The story concerns three men in a house in a street. If I could say the words I would sing the story. I would whisper it into the ears of women, of mothers. I would run through the world saying it over and over. My tongue would be torn loose. It would rattle against my lips." At a still more complex level, "A Divine Gesture" parodies the imagery, both biblical and orphic, that fills *A New Testament*. One strophe, or paragraph, in "A Thinker" exemplifies the way in which Anderson combines images from sources as diverse as Genesis and neoplatonist lore: "You are floating in a medium outside my own. That must be quite apparent. All men and women I have ever seen were floating in a medium outside my own. I a little understand the necessity for that — now. The day for the cure has not come. The time when God will breathe life into our nostrils lies lost in the future." Anderson's use of the mechanical appurtenances of modern living, which Hemingway parodies with his boot jacks and bathtubs, occurs in such a statement from "The Man with a Trumpet" as "I whispered words at night into a telephone." The orphic image of the life-stream in which all float and of which all should realize they are a part, which Anderson figures also through the image of a couple walking hand in hand, is parodied in Hemingway's fable when God and Gabriel walk up the heavenly stair hand in hand. The Great Lord God and the angel Gabriel amusingly parody the biblical element in Anderson's prose-poems. Anderson sought to lift the mundane and ordinary, the plain house in an equally plain street, the words whispered into a telephone, to the sphere of the poetic, the ideal, the mysterious; the actual and literal and local were symbolic of the ideal, the transcendental, the universal. In "A Divine Gesture,' Hemingway sought to work the opposite effect; his aim is to obtrude boot jacks and bathtubs, tycoons and yes-men into the shadowy realm of symbolist fable and thus to enforce the ironic and even pessimistic lesson of his naturalism.

In *A Moveable Feast,* Hemingway admitted that his first novel, *The Torrents of Spring,* was a parody of Sherwood Anderson's *Dark Laughter.* On a much lesser scale, "A Divine Gesture" parodied the prose-poems of *The Triumph of the Egg* and *A New Testament.* Hemingway's first appearance as a professional writer, an appearance made possible and sponsored by Anderson, was as a parodist of the man whose stories he professed to admire and who gave him a helping hand.

The next issue of *The Double-Dealer,* for June 1922, printed Hemingway's second and final contribution, "Ultimately" — four brief lines portraying the frustrating difficulty of the artist in communicating the "truth." As in the early and middle 1920's Hemingway's essential struggle as a writer was the battle to master a technique that enabled him to communicate his vision of truth, "Ultimately" is pregnant with significance for his future. Its protagonist has "tried to spit out the truth," but at first his mouth is dry, and "in the end" he merely drools and slobbers, "Truth dribbling his chin." The lines are inept and strained.

As Charles Fenton suggested, Hemingway's poems were the productions of a young man who was in the process of becoming a great prose writer. If "Ultimately" is like one of the poems that Scofield Thayer mailed back to Hemingway, the rejection only exemplifies the general soundness of Thayer's taste as an editor, and no one at *The Dial* ever need feel remorse over rejecting such writing. The publication of "Ultimately" in *The Double-Dealer* was an act of faith in the poet's future, not a signal of his achievement. Although the irony was as crude and the parodic imitativeness of Stephen Crane's poems as obvious as the pastiche of "A Divine Gesture," the rather brutal, parading masculinity is more familiar to readers of Hemingway's later work. Nor is it odd that he was, in thus seeking out pragmatically his own manner, attempting to assert it through imitating such diverse models; for the most important models for the writers of the New Movement were the aesthetes, the early naturalists, the decadents, the Bohemians of the Mauve Nineties — the writers who, opposed to the flood of popular writing in the mass-circulation magazines and papers, sought an advanced and sympathetic readership in such early little magazines as *The Chap-Book, The Yellow Book, The Lark, The Savoy.*

Indeed, the poem that was printed on the upper, and major, portion of the same page as "Ultimately" — William Faulkner's "Portrait" — would justify that observation. The author of "Portrait" was, according to "Notes on Contributors" for the issue, "William Faulkner of Oxford, Miss., . . . a young Southern poet of unusual promise," and the poem marked his literary debut. It is a much more polished and ambitious performance than "Ultimately," not a conventional love poem but a searching literary portrait in the spirit of the decadent English poets of the 1890's written to an unnamed girl whom the poet obviously was in love with. The rhetoric, the long line, adumbrate William Faulkner's later achievement in style, just as the taciturn naturalism of "Ultimately" foreshadows, say, *To Have and Have Not.* There is one obvious Americanism in "Portrait";

> Let us lightly speak at random; tonight's movie,
>   Repeat a broken conversation, word for word;
> Of friends, and happiness. The darkness scurries,
>   And we hear again a music both have heard.

It is not often that a magazine prints the earliest work of two Nobel laureates on the same page!

For Hemingway the rest of 1922 was not productive except of journalism, to which he resorted in order to support his creative work. He continued to write stories for the Sunday magazine of the *Toronto Star* and traveled in Switzerland and Spain, in Italy and Germany, for the paper and on vacations. These backgrounds soon proved to be the very stuff of the stories he began to write. In May 1922, Hemingway told Sherwood Anderson that he had been "working like hell at writing," but in the latter six months of the year he published nothing in the little magazines, and the novel he was writing then never saw the light of publication. Yet the year's efforts bore fruit, for in 1923 work by him appeared in both Harriet Monroe's *Poetry* and Margaret Anderson's *Little Review,* and, most importantly, he achieved his metier as a writer in the short prose vignettes he published in *The Little Review.*

CHAPTER 3

"FOR we have thought the longer thoughts / And gone the shorter way," begins Hemingway's little poem, "Chapter Heading," one of those that *Poetry* published:

> And we have danced to devils' tunes,
>   Shivering home to pray;
> To serve one master in the night,
>   Another in the day.

The devil in this case might well be Mammon, the god who forced Hemingway to drudge away at his articles for the *Star Weekly* and at his news stories for the *Toronto Daily Star*. With six poems appearing together in the same issue of *Poetry*, Ernest Hemingway could begin to feel that his servitude to his master of the night might come to an end and that all his service soon might be given instead to the master of the day, Apollo.

Hemingway's appearance in the issue of *Poetry* for January 1923 was his initial success as an artist. Then even more than now, *Poetry* was the most widely noticed showcase for young poets first appearing before an international readership of other poets and of cultivated readers involved in the

encouragement of what the Editor called "modern progressive art." After a decade of publication, *Poetry* was still edited
by the redoubtable spinster who had brought out its first
issue in October 1912. With its motto from Walt Whitman,
"To have great poets there must be great audiences too,"
Poetry might seem to be in the nativist, regional tradition;
Miss Monroe had famously printed Carl Sandburg's "Chicago" in the March 1914 *Poetry,* and many other poems by him
in later issues, and she had also published Vachel Lindsay's
"General William Booth Enters into Heaven" in the fourth
number of her little magazine. Actually, *Poetry* was as cosmopolitan in its sympathies as Whitman himself had been,
and as eclectic — much more eclectic in its sympathies and
critical outlook, in fact, than Ezra Pound, who for its first
six years was chief advisor as well as Foreign Correspondent
for the journal. Yet Pound acknowledged, in a letter written
for the November 1936 issue of *Poetry,* the issue of homage
and tribute to Harriet Monroe shortly after she died, that
it was to "Miss Monroe's credit that *Poetry* never degenerated
into a factional organ. Her achievement was to set up a
trade-journal in the best sense of the word." Here, in their
common respect for a craft and its discipline, the attitudes of
Pound, the Editor of *Poetry,* and Hemingway himself were
the same, whatever their other differences. Publication of his
poems in *Poetry* also meant that as a serious artist Hemingway now appeared in the little magazine that had published
such admired work as T. S. Eliot's "The Love Song of J.
Alfred Prufrock" and William Butler Yeats's "A Prayer for
My Daughter."

Grouped under the title "Wanderings" and respectively
entitled "Mitrailliatrice," "Oily Weather," "Roosevelt,"
"Riparto d'Assalto," "Champs d'honneur," and "Chapter
Heading," these six poems in *Poetry* mark the beginnings of
Hemingway's distinctive manner of expression. All are short,
and in this respect they link with the brief vignettes of the
Paris edition of *in our time,* which Hemingway began writ-
ing early in 1923. In most of these poems the influence of
Stephen Crane is, moreover, still clearly discernible, espe-
cially in the sharp distinctness and brevity with which Hem-
ingway outlined his images and metaphors; of course the
Imagists had also worked in the manner in which Crane had

pioneered, but Hemingway's combination of symbolic images and abstract commentary is in Crane's by now old-fashioned vein rather than in the more difficult exploitation of metaphor in the Imagist technique. "Champs d'honneur" with its picture of soldiers dying in battle invites comparison with Crane's "War Is Kind," although Hemingway's effort is the slighter, the more restricted in its point of view of war.

Perhaps with Horace's great line, *Dulce et decorum est pro patria mori,* in mind, Hemingway replies negatively to the suggestion that it is sweet and fitting to die for one's fatherland. "Soldiers never do die well," he asserts, and from that generalization he depicts their pitching, coughing, and twitching while all the world is roaring red and black. Stuck above their faces, wooden crosses mark the places where they have fallen in the battle:

> Soldiers smother in a ditch,
> Choking through the whole attack.

The regularity of the meter Hemingway employed here is unlike Crane's, but the leading, general comment followed by the exemplary pair of images (of the cemetery and the battle field that results in the cemetery) is the strategy Crane used. Crane's also, as much as Hemingway's, are the attitudes expressed toward death and the soldier, of stoic acceptance of the one and bitter compassion for the other.

Even more obviously like one of Crane's poems in deployment of comment and imagery and in metrical technique is the first of the six, "Mitrailliatrice." Again the poem begins with the recollection of a classical tag: "The mills of the gods grind slowly." But "this mill," the mill the narrator of the brief lyric is describing, moves jerkily, rapidly, chattering "in mechanical staccato," in a rhythm opposed to the slow inevitability of the divine laws of nature. Another image follows, explaining the mechanical quality of "this mill":

> Ugly short infantry of the mind,
> Advancing over difficult terrain,
> Make this Corona
> Their mitrailleuse.

Here Hemingway first comments on the hard craft of the writer. The writer's struggle with his material — to order it, to master it — is compared to the general's struggle with an enemy whom he must conquer; the writer's weapon is his Corona typewriter, the general's is the machine-gun; and the sound of battle, mental or physical, is the mechanical chatter of the typewriter or the machine-gun; as a general deploys his infantry to conquer difficult terrain, so the writer deploys his thoughts, the "Ugly short infantry of the mind," to win a victory over the recalcitrant raw material of nature in order to produce the finished poem. There is still another sense, a classical and theological one: "The mills of the gods grind slowly." Both the general who conceives the strategy of the battle and the writer who conceives the total poem are godlike, because they are creators bringing order out of chaos in their different ways, peace out of war, art out of nature.

The neat control of the images forecasts Hemingway's mastery of symbolic description, to be achieved within the year in his first masterpieces, the vignettes of *in our time.* "Mitrailliatrice" and "Champs d'honneur" show, too, that Hemingway was then finding the distinctive subject that brought him his first and widest fame — not so much war as men at war, men facing the crisis of their lives under the most desperate of all conditions, modern warfare. As yet, in "Wanderings," this is unfocused, Hemingway's hero is absent, the code is unformulated; but already in the longest and most circumstantial of these little pieces, "Riparto d'Assalto," one observes both a sudden advance in technique and the locale of *A Farewell to Arms.* Soldiers loaded into camions dream during the "Damned cold, bitter, rotten ride" on the "Winding road up the Grappa side." Ironically the "Pride of their country," these Arditi "stiff and cold," with their "Bristly faces, dirty hides," are thinking of a "Warm and soft and sleepy whore" back in Mestre. But the "Grey, cold, bitter, sullen ride" ends at the "splintered pines on the Grappa side / At Asalone, where the truck-load died" before reaching the battle. Here, without superfluous, generalizing commentary (the adjectives describing the ride function as the responses to their experience of the men dreaming of the whore), Hemingway for the first time exploited a technique he made peculiarly his own in his stories and novels. The poem is not in Crane's manner but in Pound's, as much an Imagist creation as Pound's famous two lines, "In A Station of the Metro," the two lines of which juxtapose the "apparition of these faces in the crowd" and a string of petals "on a wet, black bough."

The imagists were much influenced by the symbolist poets, but there is a considerable advance, in immediacy as well as in difficulty for the reader, in the Imagist effort to achieve desired effects by presenting images exactly and thus making those pictures concrete, sharply delineated, hard and clear, not blurred or diffuse as in, for example, Baudelaire's "Correspondences" and Mallarme's "L'Apres-midi d'un faune." The Imagists wished to use the exact language of common speech, to create new rhythms, to allow absolute freedom in choice of subject. To them, concentration was of the very essence of poetry. Pound led the way, in 1913, with his anthology *Des Imagistes,* the first of several such volumes annually published; but when Amy Lowell appropriated the movement to herself, Pound disavowed it, and it rapidly suffocated in Miss Lowell's weighty embrace. The dispersal of the coterie did not mark the end of Imagism, for the Imagist technical innovations were, to put the matter baldly, just too useful to be allowed to die. Of course Imagist poetry had its great weakness: the poets could not write discursively if they restricted themselves to a series of sharp, bright, relatively uncommunicative images and metaphors. Such a method constricted unbearably the range of poetic expression. Other poets, however, used Imagist techniques; for example, T. S. Eliot, in *The Waste Land,* expanded his frame of reference by using cinematic montage effects and the ancient literary devices of allusion and associative reference, so that he wrote a great didactic poem. Pound too was exploiting Imagist techniques, at about this time, in the epic scope of his early *Cantos.* It thus was not by chance that Hemingway was arriving somewhere in the vicinity of Eliot's and Pound's exploitation of Imagist techniques. What remained now was for Ernest Hemingway to drop the rhymes of poetry and the strongly emphasized musical rhythms of the new poetry of Imagism; he would carry over into prose the new freedom of choice in subject (in 1912, Miss Monroe would never have allowed "whore" in the pages of *Poetry!*) that the Imagists had fought for, and would insist, in prose, on the exact, not merely the decorative, word, in order to avoid the cliché and the trite.

In *A Moveable Feast*, Hemingway satirizes the critic, Hal, who tells him about his earliest writing that it is not only too stark but also too stripped and lean and sinewy — much the same objection Wyndham Lewis voiced in 1934, when he wrote that the "sort of First-person-singular that Hemingway invariably invokes is a dull-witted, bovine, monosyllabic simpleton." Playing along with Hal, whom he holds in contempt, Hemingway promises to fatten up his prose a bit. But he makes clear to readers of the story, "Birth of a New School," in which Hal figures that in his early writing — specifically here the Nick Adams stories — he conceives his fiction in the terms of Imagist poetry, and that its "stripped" quality is due to his use of Imagist technique. Reviewing these beginnings, he remarked that on some days his writing went so well he could create his country of upstate Michigan so that, metaphorically and imaginatively, he lived the experience he was writing about and could walk into the story, and he used the image of the hunter or hiker who walks through the tall trees to emerge into a clearing on a hill above a lake and there sees a range of hills across the water. The vista is a classic image of the discovery of a farther range of the creative imagination, one that Pope envisioned in his *Essay on Criticism* (though his hills were Alps) and that in "On First Looking into Chapman's Homer" Keats, perhaps most triumphantly of all writers, saw when his hunter-hiker, Balboa, emerged from the jungle atop a peak in Darien and discovered the shimmering South Sea limitless before him.

Even the necessary pause to sharpen his pencil became, in those hours of creative discovery, a portion of the total rhythm of Hemingway's art, so that the train of his imagining was not broken. The external act of sharpening the pencil point or cleaning the clogged sharpener was thus melded with the hiker's resumption of the pack load on his back and continuing his moccasined amble over the pine needles down to the waters of the lake: creator and creation were fused in the total act of writing, the writing of the amble was one with the walking, the search for words was one with the search for a way out of the woods on to the lake's beach.

Still another image emerges from *A Moveable Feast* to convey something of Hemingway's Imagist technique. At the beginning of 1924, after the Hemingways and their baby had returned to Paris from Toronto and Hemingway had decided to starve in order to write seriously, he got into an argument one evening with Gertrude Stein. She related to Hemingway the circumstances in which her Ford had not been repaired adequately by a young French mechanic, a veteran; his boss had said to him, "You are all a *génération perdue,*" and Miss Stein approvingly applied the stricture to Hemingway and his friends, because of their drinking, lack of discipline, the way they wrote: "That's what you all are. All of you young people who served in the war. You are a lost generation." Later when Hemingway wrote *The Sun Also Rises,* he tried to balance Miss Stein's quotation from the garage keeper with one from Ecclesiastes: "One generation passeth away, and another generation cometh; but the earth abideth forever . . . The sun also ariseth, and the sun goeth down, and hasteth to the place where he arose . . . The wind goeth toward the south, and turneth about unto the north; it whirleth about continually, and the wind returneth again according to his circuits . . . All the rivers run into the sea; yet the sea is not full; unto the place from whence the rivers come, thither they return again." But these thoughts on the abidingness of earth and the transience of man's troubles were for the future.

That night walking to his apartment on the rue Notre Dame-des-Champs, Hemingway thought about the young mechanic in the garage and whether he had ever been hauled to the front in an old Model-T Ford, like Miss Stein's, when they were converted into ambulances. Descending the mountain roads heavy with a full load of wounded soldiers, these rattling tin lizzies broke under the strain; first the brakes burned out, then the drivers braked downhill in low gear, and finally they resorted to descending in reverse gear. The last of the makeshift ambulances were driven empty over the mountainsides so that they might be replaced by newer, proper vehicles, big Fiats with a good H shift and metal-to-metal brakes. In his reverie walking home, Hemingway thought back to his conversation that evening with Gertrude Stein, to her remarks about Sherwood Anderson and the *génération perdue,* and to such abstruse yet immediate problems as egotism and mental laziness as opposed to the artist's self-discipline. Whose generation was, really, lost? Which generation of writers was, really, lazy and self-indulgent? Surely not his own, which had endured the bitter metamorphosis of the war and after, in the years of peace, had had to make lives for themselves amid the incomprehension of those who had not known the warfare of the European fronts.

Some other thoughts occur as one reads Hemingway's account. First, his difference with Gertrude Stein and Sherwood Anderson had to do with his dislike of their writing techniques as well as with their personal self-indulgences and foibles. They did not subdue themselves as craftsmen to the demands of the craft of writing, because of their egotism and mental laziness, their lack of discipline. And to Hemingway, that discipline was remarkably much the same that it was for Pound; the Imagist exploitation of the sensory datum, the keenly sensed image. Second, the image of the lost generation was not that of Gertrude Stein, the inept young artisan whose adeptness had been impaired because of the war, so that he was "lost," as an able mechanic. Rather Hemingway thought of the young soldiers who literally had been lost, had lost their lives because of the faulty mechanisms of cars not made for and unsuited to the demands of war. And this image is very close to that of Hemingway's poem in the January 1923 issue of *Poetry*, "Riparto d'Assalto." In the poem, the soldiers are killed as their camions take them upward in the mountains to the battle; in the memoir, the picture is of the soldiers in their ambulances being carried downward away from the fighting. Both images reflect Hemingway's own experience as an ambulance driver on the northern Italian battle front in June and July of 1918, and of course both images were later expanded and merged with other related images in the first three books of *A Farewell to Arms*. For Hemingway that image "spoke" for the war, and it obsessed him through most of the 1920's until he exorcized it by giving it its fullest realization in his great novel.

"News Notes" in *Poetry* for January 1923 began with a favorable notice of the latest Dial Award, that to T. S. Eliot, whose *Waste Land* had just been published in *The Dial* for November 1922, to great acclaim. Eliot had been one of the earlier successes of *Poetry*, but its Editor had never wholeheartedly responded to his poems, and for some years Eliot had sent his work to other little magazines. Miss Monroe nevertheless approved of the bestowal of the Dial Award on

Eliot. As she explained, "We are particularly interested to note that *The Dial*'s award of two thousand dollars to a young American writer had gone this year once more to a poet, T. S. Eliot. The purpose of the award, to give a young writer whose previous work has shown promise of development a chance to continue his work for a year with no financial difficulties to hamper him, is highly commendable. We congratulate *The Dial* on the significance of its choice of Mr. Eliot, and on its enlightened encouragement of modern progressive art." Hemingway's place in "News Notes" was humbler: "Ernest M. Hemingway, a young Chicago poet now abroad, will soon issue in Paris his book of verse." The most interesting gleaning from that sentence is that Hemingway already was planning the little pamphlet William Bird issued about July 1923 as *3 Stories & 10 Poems*.

Of greater interest is the evidence in "News Notes" that Hemingway was beginning to act as a collector of literary gossip, a role that he filled both in letters to Ford Madox Ford's *Transatlantic Review* and in his own fiction and books of memoirs. "News Notes" said that "A letter from Ernest Hemingway gives us all kinds of news, in brief: that Gertrude Stein is doing a new book while living in St. Remy in Provence this winter; that Ford Madox Hueffer is on his way to Paris after living on his farm in England; that James Joyce is ill and having a difficult time with his eyes; and that Padraic Colum is likewise in Paris." The evidence of this gossip places Hemingway's submission of "Wanderings" as November 1922, just before he went to Lausanne to report the peace conference held there at the close of 1922, for the *Toronto Star*. It also displays a reporter's quickly gained footing of familiarity with writers of the vanguard then living in Paris. The next paragraph of News Notes may well have come in the mail with Hemingway's letter, as an enclosure: "Ezra Pound is now connected with the Three Mountains Press, 19 rue d'Antin, which, under his editorial direction, is about to bring out books by Ford Madox Hueffer, William Carlos Williams, Ernest Hemingway and Ezra Pound. According to the printed information sent out by the Press, their aim is 'to free prose writers from the necessity of presenting their work in the stock-sized volume of commerce.'" Hemingway was, quite deliberately, already linking himself with

Gertrude Stein, Ezra Pound, James Joyce, and other writers
of the New Movement not as a mere camp-follower but as a
creator equal if not in achievement at least in intention and
promise to his new friends. In Chicago during the winter and
spring of 1921, Hemingway's older friend Y. K. Smith had
felt that Hemingway had no clear conception of what he
wanted to do, even though he had a very real notion of what
he didn't want. On the evidence of these "News Notes,"
Hemingway really wanted to become a serious writer like
Gertrude Stein, Ezra Pound, or James Joyce, if only through
the vicarious experience of associating himself with them.

In addition, the six poems in "Wanderings" show that
Hemingway was actively pursuing his ambition of becoming
a creative artist. These poems do not contain the name-drop-
ping of the item in "News Notes," but later poems — in
The Little Review, in *Der Querschnitt* — as well as his letters
and stories and editorials in the little magazines deliberately
dropped the names of men and women well known in politics
and, especially, in the arts. The repeated act must have
filled some psychic emptiness, for the names are not employed as, say, Milton used exotic and evocative names in
Paradise Lost. Hemingway also was preparing to use this
rather ordinary gossip and chit-chat in a more serious if no
more deliberate way; he was to base his first major novel, *The
Sun Also Rises,* entirely on the lives of the people whose
names he so blithely dropped in his writing for various little
magazines. *The Sun Also Rises* was in its day read with
amusement or exasperation as a *roman à clef* and still retains
interest as an example of the genre.

In such ways, Hemingway built up his image, his mental
construction of what he would like to be, what the Jungians
call the persona. Y. K. Smith, as always a shrewd observer of
Hemingway, told Dale Kramer that he felt seeds of aggression
in Hemingway and explained the statement by a theory he had
formed in observing him as boy and man. To Smith it seemed
that Hemingway had organized a private club in his head,
and that, having absolute power, he was constantly taking in
new members and casting out those who failed to meet his
standards at a given time. Anderson was needed by Hemingway and so had been taken into the club. But Anderson's
sin — as Kramer reported Smith's conversation — was that

of being larger than the founder of the club; it had accompanied him, and the mark for later slaughter was upon him. This strikes one as acute. Hemingway's reporting of gossip repeats certain names again and again. These are the insiders. The member of the group who is farthest inside is none other than the writer, the purveyor of the gossip himself. Toward the group the writer has an attitude of irony and ambivalence: its members are both glamorous and depraved (because dissipated), admirable because of their qualities of being able to withstand considerable dissipation, despised because they refuse to live by the gospel of hard work and worldly achievement. The club has a title: the Lost Generation. Hemingway is both inside the club as a member and outside the club as a kind of Jamesian observer and moralizing commentator and raisonneur.

That side of Hemingway's career has been perhaps the one most often commented upon. At the beginning, the legend he fabricated about himself was not only fashionable in itself but was widely imitated by lesser novelists and by some readers as well. In later years, however, the Hemingway legend received at best ironic comment. In 1954 Ben Hecht, comparing Sherwood Anderson and Hemingway, saw that Anderson wrote without eye to reader, critic, or royalty returns, that he looked only into himself, and that unlike most of his imitators, "of whom Ernest Hemingway was the best," he did not hitch his poetry to ten-twenty-thirty melodramas. "Unlike Hemingway *et al.*, he did not grandly play the poet while busily wooing the box office." But, then, Anderson made his own image to live up to, and just as his admirers helped him to fill out that image, so it went with Hemingway. Of the help that Ernest Hemingway received in creating his legend he enjoyed an embarrassment of riches. A representative example is that given by a fellow Chicagoan, Archibald MacLeish, in his poem "Cinema of a Man," an elegy for Harry Crosby. Gilbert Highet views this as a classic example of kitsch; it is also a contribution to the legend that Hemingway was constructing:

> He walks with Ernest in the streets in Saragossa
> They are drunk their mouths are hard they say *qué cosa*
> They say the cruel words they hurt each other
> Their elbows touch their shoulders touch their feet
> go on and on together

In two other poems MacLeish rises above such gossip, different from a Louis Sobol column of the 1920's mostly in syntax and rhyme and omission of punctuation. In these other poems, MacLeish envisions Hemingway as a legend, a vatic and fatal figure of the artist, an examplar of the age. In "Sentiments for a Dedication," MacLeish praises Hemingway as one of a band of visionaries whom the poet calls "brother"; for it was Ernest "that saw the first snow in the fox's feather." And MacLeish dedicated his "Voyage" "for Ernest Hemingway"; it is about those adventurers who sail fatally and deliberately with a cargo of "headed poppies" and "garlic longed for by the dead" traversing the westward ocean to "that island on the sea at last"

> Steep to the gull-less shore
> Across the sea rush
> Trade we our cargoes with the dead for sleep.

The theme of death is perhaps the major theme of "Wanderings," and that theme was an integral portion of the legend about himself, the golden mask, that Hemingway was making, as integral to the persona of the writer as were the images of the insider and the observer. In his poem "Roosevelt," Hemingway wrote about Theodore Roosevelt some lines that perhaps apply to his own career:

> . . . all the legends that he started in his life
> Live on and prosper,
> Unhampered now by his existence.

More than gossip about his acquaintances and himself went into the building of the Hemingway legend. Like all legends, it started with a core of fact. Yet even the fact had the outsize proportions of legend, so that apocryphal detail is much like truth. Shortly before "Wanderings" appeared in *Poetry,* Hemingway suffered the kind of loss that makes a writer's nightmare. In November 1922, as correspondent for the *Toronto Star,* he went to Lausanne to cover the peace conference held to settle the Greco-Turkish war. There he saw a good deal of one of the most famous of all American journalists, Lincoln Steffens, who had gained his fame in the employ of S. S. McClure as one of the muckrakers of *McClure's Magazine* just after the turn of the century. Steffens's confidence in Hemingway's future as a writer was immediate and certain; he read some of Hemingway's rejected manuscripts and sent one story, "My Old Man," to the editor of *Cosmopolitan* magazine, Ray Long. But Long rejected the story; Hemingway was not yet acceptable to the mass-circulation magazines.

Meanwhile, just before Christmas, Hadley Hemingway set out from Paris to join her husband for the holidays in Switzerland, for ten days of skiing and bobsledding in the mountains away from the peace conference. She packed nearly all the writing her husband had done for the past four years — what he had written during a winter in Petoskey, Michigan, in 1919, a summer and fall in Toronto in 1920, and in Chicago in 1920-21, as well as the stories and poems composed in Paris in 1922. This work had been carefully copied, classified in manila folders, and placed in a suitcase for the journey. Most importantly, there was the novel Hemingway was working on. Hadley Hemingway was bringing the material from Paris to Lausanne as a surprise, so that her husband could work on his stories during their holiday in the mountains. She brought Hemingway's uncompleted novel along, because she felt certain that he would wish to show its chapters to his new and more eminent, more experienced friend whose praises he had recently been singing in letters to Hadley — Lincoln Steffens. It was a novel that Hemingway was writing with all the lyric ease, the facility of poetic expression, of boyhood, that ease as transient and deceiving as youth itself.

In the process of getting settled into her compartment in the train for Lausanne, Hadley Hemingway left the suitcase unattended for a moment or two; and when she returned, it had vanished. So deeply had Hemingway put himself into his early writing that Hadley Hemingway thought he never recovered from the pain of that irreparable loss.

In the story "Hunger Was a Good Discipline" in *A Moveable Feast*, Hemingway described the trauma of that loss, a wound for Hadley as well as for himself. First she had wept and wept, unable to communicate the reason for her distress. Finally, persuaded by Hemingway that whatever had happened to cause such tears, nothing could be as painful as what she was undergoing, that somehow things could be worked out, Hadley confessed. One imagines Hemingway's stunned astonishment on hearing the bad news. At first he felt positive Hadley would have known better than to bring, in one suitcase, both the original typed copy and the carbon copies of those pages; but when he realized the import of her tale, he decided to go at once to Paris, to the flat, to see whether some item might be rescued from the disaster. As his reporting job enabled him to afford the luxury, he hired a replacement who would cover his dispatches to the *Star* and got on the express for Paris. But the flat in Paris held none of the missing papers. Over a third of a century after the theft, Hemingway still could not bring himself to recount what he did in the night, alone in the Paris flat, facing the numbing discovery that almost everything he had written since coming to Europe had vanished with the fatal suitcase. He could not make himself write again until he went skiing the following spring, when he wrote "Out of Season," included in *3 Stories & 10 Poems* with the two stories surviving the robbery.

After what must have been a gloomy holiday, the Hemingways went from Switzerland down to Rapallo on the Italian Riviera, where Ezra Pound had by this time established himself. In his memoir *Being Geniuses Together*, Robert McAlmon tells about his meeting with Ernest Hemingway after the catastrophe of the lost suitcase. McAlmon learned that most of Hemingway's writing had been lost but that there were some poems and stories that for one reason or another were rescued from the general calamity. There was "Up in Michigan," which had been out to *Cosmopolitan* (in 1938, in his author's preface to *The Fifth Column and the First Forty-Nine Stories*, Hemingway mistakenly said he had written it in Paris in 1921; but he must have written it in 1922 if he wrote it in Paris) ; there were the six poems of "Wanderings"; there was "My Old Man," which had been left in a drawer instead of in a suitcase (or else had been lent, fortunately, to Lincoln Steffens); there were four other poems — "Oklahoma," "Captives," "Montparnasse," and "Out of Youth" — and a third short story, "Out of Season," written after the loss of the manuscripts. McAlmon said in reminiscence, "I was publishing books in Paris and decided to do his three stories and ten poems."

McAlmon's press had been started with a gift of 14,000 pounds from his father-in-law Sir John Ellerman, who was the power behind the Cunard Line. Spurred by this largesse, McAlmon got together with a newspaperman named William Bird, who as a hobby had recently started his own small press, the Three Mountains Press, and they joined forces. According to Bird, the joining of forces extended only to distribution: "I printed a list of books in print headed 'Contact Editions, including books printed at the Three Mountains Press.' My idea was that the Three Mts. was a printing office, and that Contact Editions was a publishing house. McAlmon, with his usual distaste for fine distinctions, never understood the arrangement and put both imprints on both his subsequent books," *Distinguished Air* (1925) and *Portrait of a Generation* (1926).

Bird too had got onto Hemingway; they had met when both were covering the Genoa Economic Conference in 1922. Hemingway then had suggested that Bird get in touch with Ezra Pound, who was working on a long poem. Bird did so, and the upshot was that Pound came up with a series of six books ("long" books, said Bird inaccurately) to be published in a series that went together rather than just a bunch of things printed as they came along; Pound thus became editor of the Three Mountains Press. The six books Bird printed were Pound's *Indiscretions or une revue de deux mondes*, Ford Madox Ford's *Men and Women*, B. C. Windeler's *Elimus: a story* (with twelve illustrations by Dorothy Shakespear, Pound's wife), William Carlos Williams's *The Great American Novel*, B. M. G. Adam's *England*, and Ernest Hemingway's *in our time*. It took an ungodly long time to get the printing done, as Bird had to work at his seventeenth-century hand press in his spare time. Bird's version of the story is that as Hemingway's book was the last on the list, he got very impatient and gave another manuscript to McAlmon, who thus got out *3 Stories & 10 Poems* a few months before *in our time*. That is to say, *3 Stories & 10 Poems* was published in the summer of 1923, probably July, while *in our time* did not come from the Three Mountains Press until January 1924.

In 1951, Hemingway denied meeting McAlmon in Rapallo, and it may just be that William Bird's account is more accurate than McAlmon's. *A Moveable Feast* is not helpful at this point. At any rate, *3 Stories & 10 Poems* represents earlier work than does *in our time* and thus marks a

transition in Ernest Hemingway's writing, from the first stories and poems, in which he was groping his way toward his
metier as an artist, to his achieved hard, "stripped" manner,
the manner of an Imagist in prose. There accordingly seems
to be a change in Hemingway's very method of composition.
Viking Press's Compass Books Edition of Charles Fenton's
Apprenticeship of Ernest Hemingway has a front-cover illustration depicting Ernest Hemingway using a typewriter by
means of the hunt-and-peck system. "Mitrailliatrice," his
first poem of "Wanderings," compares a soldier's conquering
machine-gun with a writer's conquering Corona typewriter;
as the ugly short infantry of the mind advances over its difficult terrain, their weapon chatters in mechanical staccato.
There is not a single similar recollection in *A Moveable
Feast*: throughout the stories, Hemingway dwells in detail
on his method of writing, a method quite deliberately designed to exploit the hard, precise, spare detail of the Imagist
metaphor, in which the artist makes each word count individually and forcefully.

For example, in the beginning story of *A Moveable Feast*,
"A Good Café on the Place St.-Michel," Hemingway no sooner
has seated himself at a table in this warm, clean, and friendly
retreat than he takes out his notebook from his jacket pocket
and begins to compose a story, writing with a pencil. Fittingly
he is writing about his *pays* of upstate Michigan, a story
in which two boys in their teens, Bill and the boy that
was Hemingway but was named Nick Adams, are drinking. (This would be the Nick Adams story entitled "The
Three-Day Blow.") Almost two pages are devoted to the
physical method of writing his story and to the psychology of
the writer in relation to his physical surroundings and also
to the harmony established between the writer, his environment of the Parisian café, and the kind of artistic expression
possible there because of his way of working — of writing
with a pencil into a notebook. As Hemingway tells us, he
made even the task of sharpening a pencil a part of the total
act of self-expression, self-realization. In his best moments, he
attained such a state that the stories wrote themselves and he
had a hard time keeping up with them. These accounts indicate an immersion in the evolving work and a rhythm like
that of a ritual, a balletic act such as the matador's encounter

with the bull in the ring. External evidence supports Hemingway's remembered description; for example, early in 1925, an editor indicates that Hemingway had his stories transcribed on the typewriter by someone else. A natural rhythm thus replaced the mechanical staccato, the chattering bursts, of the reporter's Corona, and the artist consciously emerged.

As an artist, Hemingway was finding his way precociously, but achieving public recognition was a more arduous job. For the rest of 1923, he published his experiments in the one little magazine that would grant them space, *The Little Review*.

The Little Review had been founded in 1914 by Margaret Anderson, its editor ever since. In 1918 she moved her journal from Chicago, where it had started its hectic career, to New York's Greenwich Village by way of a brief detour in the purlieus of San Francisco. In the Village the proprietress, along with her sidekick Jane Heap, occasionally went hungry, but her journal soared to renown and notoriety. Amid much publicity, a court action extending from the summer of 1920 through February 1921 resulted in Margaret Anderson's being fined and her journal's temporary suppression because she had published serially most of James Joyce's morally scandalous and aesthetically modernist novel, *Ulysses*. The publication of *Ulysses* would, alone, gain Miss Anderson a place in the annals of the little magazine; her standing trial because of that publication gained her martyrdom. Devoted to the vanguard, she published everything from the mad lucidity of the Baronin Elsa von Freytag-Loringhoven's prose and poetry to the tirades of Jane Heap, whose customary weapon resembled not so much a pen as an executioner's axe, from T. S. Eliot and Jean Cocteau to Sherwood Anderson and Gertrude Stein. At its silliest, *The Little Review* aired such experiments as R. Huelsenbeck's "Les Primitifs," translated by the young Surrealist, Louis Aragon:

> "indigo indigo
> "tramway sac de sommeil
> "Punaise et puce
> "indigo indiga"
>   "oumbaliska
>   "boum DADAî

What the philistines thought was irrelevant. The art of

the younger generation must be served. Margaret Anderson and Jane Heap prided themselves on their independence and on their interest in all the groupings and regroupings within the New Movement. Toward the close of its career, *The Little Review* for Spring 1926 declared in "Notes on Contributors," àpropos the Surrealists, that in America there was a prejudice, a disdain even, "for groups, cliques, revolutions, movements, in fact for all of the tricks that the young Europeans make use of to ward off blight and boredom." The editor announced that her magazine always welcomed "these signs of life and without fear of contagion and not heavily we have published the work of the entire first line of the foremost artists in Europe. In fact, we have unostentatiously presented all of the new systems of art to America . . . about twenty Isms, in the past few years." America was, it appeared, all too serious about art, so serious that "we treat it as we treat the dead," with respect and no attempt at communication. As long as such an attitude obtained, *The Little Review* saw little hope for art in America. "If groups, cliques, revolutions, movements, tricks will change this we are for groups, cliques, etc."

For fifteen years *The Little Review* did indeed fight off the blight of boredom. Its best was the best of the most glamorous decade in America's history: *Ulysses,* of course; such of Eliot's poems, after *Poetry* turned against him, as "The Hippopotamus" and "Sweeney among the Nightingales"; much of Pound's critical writing, his important review of C. H. Douglas's *Economic Democracy,* and many poems; stories, poems, essays from Jean Cocteau; Wallace Stevens's poems; Hart Crane's "Voyages" I and II; and contributions from persons as widely various as Herwarth Walden (whose Berlin *Sturm* was spiritual cousin to *The Little Review*), Henry Blackman Sell, Émile Verhaeren, Marsden Hartley, Ben Hecht, Tristan Tzara, the Anarchist Emma Goldman (*The Little Review* endured its anarchist phase in, appropriately, Chicago). There was even a hoax poem, "Opus 96" by the "Spectrist" poet Emanuel Morgan, Witter Bynner's name assumed for the perpetration of the hoax. *The Little Review* published reproductions of the work of Picasso, Brancusi, Marie Laurencin, Man Ray, Stuart Davis, Max Ernst, Fernand

Léger, Francis Picabia, the Russian Constructivist artists —
and of course much of Dada.

By 1922 existence in New York meant the struggle to
secure generous patrons in the face of the relentless, demean-
ing publicity bestowed on her review and the editor herself,
undernourishment, and poverty in the face of a curious and
undying fame. Margaret Anderson's life took on the aspect of
a polar expedition, all life serving only to maintain life. The
magazine she had started as a monthly had slowed down to
the pace of a quarterly, and even that pace of publication
had become irregular and uncertain. She wanted to escape
by getting a job and thus supporting *The Little Review*. Jane
Heap opposed this resolve and argued that it was going over
to the enemy, so Margaret Anderson drudged on until, she
said, "I did a nervous breakdown that lasted many months."
At that juncture and at John Quinn's home, she met William
Butler Yeats; so entranced was she by Yeats's stories about
the people in Europe she wanted to know that she suddenly
found the key to her discontent: "It was the time to go to
Europe." And Europe was made possible by Georgette Leblanc, the singer and actress who had at one time been
Maurice Maeterlinck's wife. Mme. Leblanc was on a tour
in America that had more downs than ups, but she generously invited Margaret Anderson to spend the summer
at her rented house in Bernardsville, New Jersey, where they
were to live "exclusively on music." Other members of the
ménage were Allen Tanner the pianist and George Antheil
the composer, at that time still a student at the Bok Con-
servatory in Philadelphia. This, then, was Margaret Anderson's opportunity to begin a pianistic career by playing accom-
paniments for Georgette Leblanc on a forthcoming European
tour.

It turned out that Jane too decided to go to Europe, and
instead of dying, *The Little Review* moved with its proprietors to Paris. First, Margaret Anderson went with Jane Heap
to see Ezra Pound, their foreign editor; then came meetings with James Joyce and Gertrude Stein, Constantin Brancusi and Francis Picabia, Eric Satie and a host of Dadaists.
There were visits to the performances of the Swedish Ballet
and the Ballets Russes of Serge Diaghilev, to Jean Cocteau's
new night club Le Boeuf sur le toit, to the Soirées de Paris

presented by the Comte de Beaumont, to marvelously riotous
Dadaist evenings at the Théâtre Michel, and to Pound's
opera *Villon* when it was performed at the old Salle Pleyel.

May 1923 was one of those springs when everyone was in
Paris, a wonderful spring. Naturally Margaret Anderson
called on the Hemingways, going with Jane Heap to dine
with them in their small apartment on the Left Bank. Hemingway read a story that evening: "It was one of the first
stories he had written — he had not yet found a publisher. I
took it," said Margaret Anderson, "immediately for the *Little
Review* and it was brought out later in his first collection,
'In Our Time.' A few months after his first appearance in
the *Little Review* we printed the second story of his to be
accepted anywhere," his "Mr. and Mrs. Elliot," in Miss Anderson's opinion, "a gem of a story."

In her opinion, also, Hemingway was soft-hearted, fell
in love too easily and too frequently for his own good, and
had a native generosity. Her single adjective for him was
"simple"; Jane, however, described their author as "a rabbit — white and pink face, soft brown eyes that look at you
without blinking." As for his love for boxing and bullfighting — all that was thrashing up the ground with his hind legs.

Whatever the accuracy of the analogy between Hemingway and a rabbit, Miss Anderson's memory slipped when she
recounted his contributions to *The Little Review*. To its
number for May 1923 he gave six of the eighteen vignettes
that constituted all of William Bird's Paris edition of *in our
time,* and less notably, a poem commenting on the Genoa
Conference he had reported in 1922 for the *Toronto Star,*
"They All Made Peace — What Is Peace?"

Of his three appearances in literary journals thus far, this
was much the most auspicious. His six paragraphs entitled
"In Our Time" led off an issue that the editor of *The Little
Review* called the Exiles number "because all of the contributors are at present pleasantly exiled in Europe." Although it was Ezra Pound's idea, the editors had nothing in
the issue to represent him. As for T. S. Eliot, he was "too
obsessed by the difficulties of the material situation" (even
though by this time Eliot had been enriched by the Dial
Award of two thousand dollars!), and Wyndham Lewis was
"busy on an exhibition and a new book." Three contributors

in the Exiles number were not American: Fernand Léger, Joan Miro, and Jean Cocteau, "the only and perfect Jean Cocteau in existence." The American contributors included Gertrude Stein, with a group of prose pieces entitled "Idem the Same," the first of which was "A Valentine to Sherwood Anderson"; E. E. Cummings, with three untitled poems; Mina Loy, with a long experimental piece of writing, "Anglo-Mongrels and the Rose," the first of two parts the magazine published; and George Antheil, with a page of the score of Section 3 of his *Airplane Sonata*. That Hemingway's Imagist vignettes led off such a company is evidence enough of the impression he made on Margaret Anderson and Jane Heap.

The word *vignette*, used by Charles Fenton to describe these six prose sketches, precisely applies to them; it is much more exact than Hemingway's own title, of "chapter," which he gave to these six and the dozen other similar sketches of the Paris edition of *in our time*. For a vignette is, in the engraver's art (and by extension, in photography), a picture that shades off gradually into the surrounding ground or the unprinted paper; thus in writing a vignette is a brief word picture, a sketch. Each of the vignettes published in *The Little Review* was later published in the same order in the Paris edition of *in our time*. This order, in which Hemingway composed them, is no longer the order in which most readers know them in the collected stories, *The Fifth Column and the First Forty-Nine Stories;* here the war vignettes are placed first, whether they derive from Hemingway's direct experience as a soldier at the Italian front or from his reporting and the stories his friends told him about the first World War and the Greco-Turkish War. As five of the vignettes Margaret Anderson published are about these two wars, their order is not greatly disturbed in the collected stories; only the second vignette in *The Little Review*, about bullfighting, is transferred to the later pages of the collected stories, and in the Paris edition of *in our time* it retained its place as the second vignette. The first vignette is a recollection by a veteran of the fighting on the French front; as a kitchen corporal, he was going to the Champagne front, and everybody was drunk, even the lieutenant. The adjutant worried about the camp kitchen, although the battery was fifty kilometers from the front: "It was funny going along that road."

In his fine book, *The Apprenticeship of Ernest Hemingway,* Charles Fenton has devoted an entire chapter to a close reading of the other five vignettes *The Little Review* published — a tough American tourist's slangy account of the bloody triumph of a young matador over eight bulls (reduced to five bulls in the collected stories); a reporter's picture of Greek peasants from Turkey being herded to Greece by the Greek army, as a result of the Greco-Turkish War; two vignettes of Mons portraying the fighting in the city and at the "river" (Mons is at the junction of the Canal du Centre and the Condé-Mons Canal) between the Germans and the British in August 1914, as related by a British officer (the second of these vignettes was uniquely designated "MONS (Two)"); and another reporter's piece, this one depicting the execution by a firing squad of six Greek cabinet ministers "at half-past six in the morning against the wall of a hospital."

Of the six vignettes, only the recounting of the flight of the Greek refugees is Hemingway's firsthand rendition of an observed experience. Charles Fenton has shown in detail that the sketch had its beginning in a dispatch Hemingway sent the *Toronto Star* and printed in its issue for October 20, 1922. The vignette in *The Little Review* was a second version of the reported experience. It was of course a greatly condensed and much more consciously artful sketch than the news story, a picture rather than a story. Hemingway revised it slightly for *in our time.* Where in *The Little Review* "Greek cavalry rode hard on the procession" of fleeing peasants, in the volume the cavalry "herded along the procession," a detail giving a very different impression of the peasants and their protectors. Such revisions, exclusive of a few changes in punctuation, are only eight in number; seven involve changes in wording, one is the excision of a phrase ("The first matador got the horn through his sword hand and the crowd hooted him on his way to the infirmary" survives in the collected stories, less vindictively, without "on his way to the infirmary"). Fenton has identified three of the narrators besides Hemingway. One was Hemingway's friend Eric Edward Dorman-Smith, a professional British soldier, who "spoke" the two Mons vignettes. The young matador's victory was spoken by an unnamed tourist from Chicago, nicknamed the Gin Bottle King by Hemingway and his friend Mike Strater, whom they sat with one afternoon at the bull ring in Madrid and talked with that night in a little restaurant. Not until October 20, 1923, did Hemingway report the story in a piece for the *Star Weekly*; his enumeration of the number of bulls the "kid" — actually a matador named Chicuelo — killed tallies with the version of the vignette *The Little Review* printed. His picture of the assassination of the Greek cabinet ministers was related to Hemingway by an American movie cameraman named Shorty Wornall; Wornall appears in a news story by Hemingway that the *Star* published on November 14, 1922. That Hemingway was thinking of the modulations of the speech of the people he knew, and knew fairly well, accounts in part for the remarkable impact each vignette makes on the reader. But the speeches of these individuls are remolded to the demands of Imagist technique, so that the end result is not the simulacrum of a taped transcript but has the stripped, hard clarity, as Edmund Wilson would soon remark, of a Goya engraving or lithograph.

In the same Exiles number of *The Little Review* appeared, some pages later on, a poem by Hemingway, "They All Made Peace — What Is Peace?," a satirical impression of the Lausanne Conference of November 1922 — January 1923. In *vers libre* strophes — very free indeed with their libelous innuendoes about details of diplomatic life — Hemingway gives what is on the surface an artless bit of tittle-tattle related in a parody of the styles of Gertrude Stein and a child's primer. As in the six vignettes in that issue, his attempt was to catch a tone, a particular voice. The voice is Hemingway's, but it is his voice mimicking other voices, whether the reporter's questions in an interview at a press conference or, at the bar of the Hotel Beau-Rivage on Lake Geneva, the fragmented chatter of shabby gossip about the diplomats and politicians drafting the terms of the peace settlement.

Hemingway was very busy there. Secret diplomacy, high-pressure tactics, slanted communiques were the order of the day. He attended a frantic series of press conferences, checked the stories and hand-outs that as often as not were deliberately conflicting in their defense of national interests, and converting his information into cabelese, sent out a morning wire to the Universal News Service and an evening wire to the International News Service. He naturally paid the greatest attention to the British press releases and daily press conferences, but he also checked the French and Turkish communiques each afternoon. Ordinarily he filed his last dispatch around three in the morning and left another with his concierge to open the wire with at seven the same morning. Out of the conference came two major stories bearing Hemingway's by-line, the first one an interview with Mussolini, "The Biggest Bluff in Europe" in the *Toronto Daily Star* for January 27, 1923, the other about the Russian commissar of foreign affairs, Georgi Tchitcherin, mailed by Hemingway on January 25, 1923, and printed in the *Star* for February 10. Hemingway's attitude toward Mussolini was candidly hostile; his attitude toward Tchitcherin was respectful of the diplomat's cold brain, inhuman capacity for work, and indifference to publicity, public opinion, money "or anything except his work and Russia," but contemptuous of Tchitcherin's vanity and his "dislike and distrust of women."

In *Poetry* for February 1931, in a long manifesto entitled "Program: 'Objectivists' 1931," Louis Zukofsky (who was special editor for the issue) reprinted "They All Made Peace — What Is Peace?" as an example of the kind of poetry he was calling for, "as good now as it was in *The Little Review* in 1922" (*sic*). And Charles Fenton has summed up its lines and themes as "forceful and precocious":

> All of the turks are gentlemen and Ismet Pasha is a
> Little deaf. But the Armenians. How about the
> Armenians?
> Well, the Armenians.
> Lord Curzon likes young boys.
> So does Chicherin.
> So does Mustapha Kemal. He is good looking too. His eyes
> Are too close together but he makes war. . .

But, said the narrator philosophically, that was the way Kemal was. And the gossip continued with the information that Lord Curzon did not love Chicherin, who thought all the time. Lord Curzon thought, too, but he was fashionable rather than coldly intellectual and preferred to go to St.

Moritz. The voice of the poem chatted on about the hatless-
ness of the American representative to the conference, Richard Washburn Child, and Baron Hyashi, the Japanese delegate, getting out of his automobile. The voice relayed apparently random and artless bits of information, bits that were,
however, not at all random but were instead deliberately
placed sharp little images that jostled side by side to form a
comprehensive picture of the conference:

> Monsieur Barrère gets telegrams. So does Marquis
>   Garonni.
> His telegrams come on motorcycles from MUSSOLINI.
> MUSSOLINI has nigger eyes and a bodyguard, and has
> His picture taken reading a book upside down.
>   MUSSOLINI is
> Wonderful. Read *The Daily Mail.*
> I used to know MUSSOLINI. Nobody liked him then.
>   Even I
> Didn't like him. He was a bad character. Ask Monsieur
>   Barrère.
> We all drink cocktails. Is it too early to have a cocktail?
> How about a drink George? Come on and we'll have a
>   cocktail,
> Admiral. Just time before lunch.. Well what if we do?
>   Not too dry.
> Well. what do you boys know this morning?
> O they're shrewd. They're shrewd.

All this is the casual, tough talk of a big hotel's bar. Everybody is agreeably stewing in the same pot, no better than he
should be and certainly no better than his fellows lounging
against the bar itself. One catches the names of the Bulgarian
dictator, Alexander Stambuliski, and the Greek politician,
Eleutherios Venizelos — who, says the voice, was "wicked"
("You can see it. His beard shows it"). But the wife of the
American delegate, Mrs. Child, was decidedly not wicked;
virtuously she had flat breasts

>   and Mr. Child is an idealist and wrote
> Harding's campaign speeches and calls Senator
>   Beveridge Al.
> You know me Al.
> Lincoln Steffens is with Child. The big C makes the
>   joke easy.

Then there was Mosul, warned the voice, and the Greek
Patriarch. "What about the Greek Patriarch?" asked the
poem in conclusion, its superficially pointless question emphasizing, actually (by hinting at another dimension of
reality), the corruption and futility of the conference and its
intrigues.

One qualifies Fenton's further remark that the antagonism Hemingway displayed in the poem embraces his own
vocation as well as diplomacy. He wrote several similar satires
in the early 1920's; this was neither the first he published nor
the last, nor is journalism scourged more savagely than other
walks of life. This poem is no harder on politics than Hemingway's earlier "Roosevelt" that *Poetry* published, and no
harder on Hemingway's circle of acquaintance than "The Soul
of Spain with McAlmon and Bird the Publishers," serialized
in *Der Querschnitt* in October-November 1924. Fenton says
also that "Hemingway's obligation to Gertrude Stein was in
this case a large one," but the influences on the poem are
more various than he suggests. First, the political orientation,
the condescension toward the diplomats and reporters, the
mingling of public issues and private lives owe something to
the content and manner of Ezra Pound's *Cantos* and *Hugh
Selwyn Mauberly*. In the section "Yeux Glauques" of the
latter poem, the allusive coupling of names with topical gossip
has its echoes.

> Gladstone was still respected,
> When John Ruskin produced
> "King's Treasuries"; Swinburne
> And Rossetti still abused.
> Foetid Buchanan lifted up his voice
> When that faun's head of hers
> Became a pastime for
> Painters and adulterers.

In Hemingway's poem, the mosaic effect of the bits of chatter from bar and press conference may not actually anticipate the similar effect for which *The Waste Land* is famous,
but both poems are interestingly close in times of composition; Eliot's was published in *The Dial* for November 1922
(distributed, however, in October) and in the first issue of
Eliot's own quarterly, *The Criterion*, for Autumn 1922.
Through his friendship with Pound and reading of the little

magazines, Hemingway was aware of Eliot's technique. Pound also wrote in the same way, and Hemingway no doubt had encountered such a passage as the following from Pound's "Sixth Canto," published in *The Dial* in August 1921:

> The Elysée carries a name on
> And the bus behind me gives me a date for peg;
> Low ceiling and the Erard and the silver,
> These are in "time." Four chairs, the bow-front dresser,
> The pannier of the desk, cloth top sunk in.
>   "Beer-bottle on the statue's pediment!
> "That, Fritz, is the era, to-day against the past,
> "Contemporary." And the passion endures.
> Against their action, aromas. Rooms, against chronicles.

The juxtaposition of the bits of conversation, the objects, the scenes, the languages is a development of Imagist technique familiar enough in the writing of Eliot and Pound; the juxtapositions as well as the images contribute to the symbolic structure of meaning. Hemingway's exploitation of this technical innovation is used effectively in "They All Made Peace — What Is Peace?" In 1936, in "The Snows of Kilimanjaro" he returned to the same technique and adapted it to the purposes of that masterpiece of his later fiction; while the story obviously owes something to the stream-of-consciousness prose of Hemingway's friend James Joyce, it also represents a further development of a kind of writing Hemingway had experimented with in early 1923.

Almost a year after the Lausanne Conference, in a letter dated November 25, 1923, Hemingway told Edmund Wilson that "They All Made Peace — What Is Peace?" was a "joke." He wrote it "in the wagon-restaurant going back to Lausanne, [from Paris, after he] had been at a very fine lunch at Gertrude Stein's and talked there all afternoon and read a lot of her new stuff and then drank a big bottle of Beaune myself in the dining car." Facing the task of opening the Universal News Service wire back to the States in the morning, he tried to analyze the conference. Hemingway tried to distil an impression of its essential quality by writing his poem in the superficially disjointed, flat, childishly direct statements of Gertrude Stein. "Her method," he told Wilson, "is invaluable for analysing anything or making notes on a person or a place. She has a wonderful head." But the neo-Imagist method of Pound and

Eliot was equally invaluable for this and other verse satires
Hemingway wrote in those years.

Besides the influences of international politics, reporting, and the writing techniques of Gertrude Stein, T. S. Eliot,
and Ezra Pound, there is also the influence of the Hemingways' domestic habits. Robert McAlmon said that in these
years of his first marriage, "Hemingway and his then wife
had a fondness for pet names, which they called each other,
baby, and their puppy. Beery-poppa (Hemingway) said a
loving good-bye to Feather-kitty (Mrs. Hemingway), Bumby
(baby), and waxen-puppy, and he and I well lubricated with
whisky got into the train," for their trip to Madrid in 1924.
In both "They All Made Peace — What Is Peace?" and "The
Soul of Spain with McAlmon and Bird the Publishers" the
style that parodies a children's primer grew from the self-
parodying domestic prattle of Hadley and Ernest Hemingway when they set up housekeeping in their apartment just off
the Place du Tertre. The mock-infantile burlesque of the
satire has its beginnings in family colloquies that themselves
were conscious parodies of other, more seriously spoken family
dialogues carried on in baby-talk.

The acceptance of his work by *The Little Review* and
by *Poetry*, the publication of *3 Stories & 10 Poems*, and the
anticipated publication of *in our time* made 1923 an auspicious year for Ernest Hemingway. He returned to Toronto
and the *Star* early in the fall of that year, to write for the
Star Weekly the interviews and special stories at which he had
become adept, and for which he received the excellent salary
of $125 a week. In October, in Toronto, John — the Bumby
of Robert McAlmon's anecdote about the Hemingways' baby-
talk — was born. But in January 1924 Hemingway had become
so discontented with his job with the *Star* that he threw it
over and made the great leap into the future that he must
make in order to realize his ambition — to create masterpieces. Hadley, Mr. Bumby, and Beery-poppa steamed back
to Europe and to Paris just in time to miss the publication of
in our time in January 1924. Having left his well-paying job,
Hemingway now must subsist on what he could earn from the
little magazines while at the same time he immersed himself
in the task of learning to master his chosen craft.

His decision, while hard, was not a rash one. He was

already gaining the recognition he must have both to justify himself as an artist and to support, eventually, his family. The Sunday edition of the *New York Tribune* on October 21, 1923, carried a note about Hemingway, written by Burton Rascoe for his feature, "A Bookman's Day Book"; Rascoe had left Chicago to become literary editor of the *Tribune* and thus was one of the most important reviewers and literary journalists in America. His "Day Book" related that he had called on Edmund Wilson and his wife late one afternoon and that "Wilson called my attention to some amusing stuff by Ernest Hemingway in the new issue of 'The Little Review.' " As Wilson notes in his essay on the "Emergence of Ernest Hemingway" — a compendium of correspondence and book review printed in his *Shores of Light* — these contributions were the six vignettes and "They All Made Peace — What Is Peace?" from the Exiles number of *The Little Review*. Rascoe continued his paragraph with the remark that Lewis Galantière had sent him a copy of *3 Stories & 10 Poems,* "which was published in Paris, and said that I would find it interesting, but I have not yet got around to reading it."

From Toronto Hemingway wrote Edmund Wilson on November 11, 1923, saying that in "Burton Rascoe's Social and Literary Notes" he had seen the notice of Wilson's kindness: "you had drawn his attention to some writing of mine in *The Little Review.*" He sent along a copy of *3 Stories & 10 Poems* and devoted the rest of his letter to the difficulties, caused partly by his isolation in Canada, he was having in getting his little book reviewed. Gertrude Stein had written that she had done a review, but Hemingway didn't know whether it had been published (it never saw publication). He wanted to send out copies for review but did not know whether to put in a dedication, "as compulsory in France, or what. Being an unknown name and the books [of Contact Editions] unimposing they would probably be received as by Mr. Rascoe who had not yet had time, after three months, to read the copy Galantiere sent him. (He could read it all in an hour and a half.)" Hemingway hoped Wilson liked the book: "If you are interested could you send me the names of four or five people to send it to to get it reviewed? It would be terribly good of you."

Edmund Wilson realized as keenly as did Hemingway

that getting one's work reviewed — sympathetically if possible, but at any rate mentioned — is vital to a writer, especially to a writer just beginning his career, whose work, because it is experimental, benefits from detailed and sympathetic attention. Wilson acknowledged receiving *3 Stories & 10 Poems* and mentioned that he might do a note on it in the "Briefer Mention" section of one-paragraph, unsigned reviews that *The Dial* published each month. Since writers as various as F. Scott Fitzgerald, Gertrude Atherton, and Ezra Pound were reviewed in "Briefer Mention," and since *The Dial* was generally if sometimes grudgingly agreed to be the leading literary journal of the vanguard, Wilson was offering to help Hemingway in a most important way. (Obviously he was not aware that Scofield Thayer had rejected Hemingway's poems early the previous year.)

Hemingway's reply, dated November 25, 1923, is all the more interesting because, while he thanked Wilson "ever so much for the letter. It was awfully good," and while he apologized for the "silly size" of the book, he asked for the greater favor of a full-dress review in *The Dial*. "Would it perhaps be better to postpone the 'Briefer Mentions' in the *Dial* until *In Our Time* comes out sometime next month and I will send it to you. You can get from it what I am trying to get at and the two of them together could make one review." He flattered Wilson rather crudely: "I am very glad you liked some of it. As far as I can think at the minute yours is the only critical opinion in the States I have any respect for. Mary Colum is sometimes sound. Rascoe was intelligent about Eliot," probably because of his reservations about *The Waste Land*. And as with Eliot, Hemingway expressed an adverse judgement on Anderson, whose work "seems to have gone to hell, perhaps from people in New York telling him too much how good he was. Functions of criticism. I am very fond of him" — he had just said he had known Anderson pretty well but had not seen him for "several years" (less than two!) — and he "has written good stories." Still, Anderson had to be put down and Hemingway's independence asserted. Wilson had quizzed Hemingway as to whether "My Old Man" in *3 Stories & 10 Poems* derived from Anderson's similar fiction, such as "I Want to Know Why," and received a blunt, definite answer: Hemingway's story derived "from boys and horses. Anderson derives from boys and horses. I don't think they're anything alike. I know I wasn't inspired by him."

Hemingway emphasized his hopes for *in our time*: "I am awfully glad you liked the *In Our Time* stuff in the *Little Review* and it is where I think I have gotten hold of it," but he added there was no use "trying to explain it without the book." Significantly — in view of Hemingway's hopes of a friendly notice from Wilson — none of the correspondence mentioned Hemingway's ten poems, nor was his appearance in *Poetry* alluded to. In the event, his judgment about *in our time* was altogether justified, and his frank courting of Wilson as a critic reaped its rich reward in 1924.

As Hemingway inferred in his letter, Edmund Wilson was not a lone resource. L. A. G. Strong, the Irish poet and novelist, printed the poem "Chapter Heading" from *Poetry*'s January 1923 issue in his anthology volume, *Best Poems of 1923*. And, more importantly, Edward J. O'Brien, the editor of the standard annual reprint anthology of short fiction, re-printed "My Old Man," the third story in *3 Stories & 10 Poems*, in his *Best Short Stories of 1923*. O'Brien had read the story early in 1923, in Rapallo, just after Hemingway's loss of his manuscripts. The story evidently made a deep impression; for in his letter of November 25, Hemingway told Wilson that O'Brien had written "the other day asking formal permission to reprint *My Old Man* in his *Best Short Stories of 1923* and asking if he could dedicate the book to me." As O'Brien's anthology wasn't out yet, "that is confidential. He prints bum ones and good ones. He asked me if I had enough stories for a Boni and Liveright book. I don't know whether that means he could get them to publish it"; and Hemingway said he would ask Wilson, who also had offered help in getting a book before the publishers, about the matter when the time came. Hemingway proudly recalled O'Brien's re-quest in *A Moveable Feast* and pointed out that O'Brien broke all his own rules against taking unpublished fiction — "My Old Man" had not been published before he selected it — in order to include the story in *Best Short Stories of 1923*. More-over, as Hemingway assured Edmund Wilson, the volume was dedicated to himself, and even though in the dedication, table of contents, and signature of authorship Hemingway

appeared as "Ernest Hemenway," the compliment was astonishing enough to treasure the rest of one's life.

The year 1923 had begun with Hemingway's appearance
in *Poetry* just after the catastrophe of Hadley Hemingway's
loss of almost all his writing; except for some poems, "My
Old Man" and "Up in Michigan" were the twin survivors of
that theft. But the year ended with the genuine promise of
better things.

CHAPTER 4

"OH here you are," said Ford Madox Ford, breathing heavily through his bristly tobacco-stained mustache. Holding himself as erect as though he were still in his officer's uniform of the first World War, he asked Ernest Hemingway, "May I sit with you?" Whether Ford realized it or not, his remark was unfortunate, for Hemingway had come to the Closérie des Lilas to have a quiet late-afternoon apéritif at a table outside and to relax as he took in the scene of the boulevard in the golden sunlight of autumn in Paris. In Hemingway's view, Ford Madox Ford resembled no officer but rather a walking, sprucely dressed hogshead on end, and he smelled, too. Hemingway avoided looking directly at Ford whenever possible and held his breath when they were together in a room without ventilation; yet the meeting outdoors this afternoon could not spoil his pleasure in his drink and in the spectacle of the changing light of autumn, and the leaves drifting downward.

In such a crisis as his disappointment at the present meeting, Hemingway dutifully tried to keep in mind Ezra Pound's chiding advice: one must never be rude to Ford, Ford lied only when he was very tired, he was really an excellent writer, he had had to endure some very trying domestic trouble. And Hemingway did his best to hold these good thoughts even though the heavy, wheezing, ignoble presence of Ford himself, barely touching-distance away, made doing so difficult. Still, one tried, for Ezra's sake. Hemingway's response to Ford's company on that afternoon and many others he summed up, in a telling image, to Gertrude Stein and Alice Toklas. After Ford came over to Paris from London to establish *The Transatlantic Review*, he came to see Gertrude Stein frequently. "I had a weakness for him," admitted Alice Toklas; but Hemingway called him the golden walrus, and in the story "Ford Madox Ford and the Devil's Disciple" in *A Moveable Feast*, Ford, with his washed-out blue eyes under colorless lids and eyebrows is portrayed as a washed-out, washed-up barrel of social pretension. As so often is the case in Hemingway's memoir, the challenging, polemic image is more complex than it appears to be on a first, casual reading.

Ford Madox Ford spoiled Ernest Hemingway's late afternoon musings, yet he was, all the same, a friend as helpful as Sherwood Anderson, Ezra Pound, and Gertrude Stein. For in 1924 it was Ford who helped Ernest Hemingway to literary prominence, not Sherwood Anderson through *The Double-Dealer*, not Margaret Anderson with her *Little Review* and Harriet Monroe with her *Poetry*, not even Robert McAlmon and William Bird and Ezra Pound with the two pamphlets of *3 Stories & 10 Poems* and *in our time*. *in our time* was published in January 1924, and back in Paris from his months in Toronto, back in Paris with Hadley and young Bumby to support, Hemingway had high hopes for the eighteen vignettes that, in the manner of a Byzantine saint's legend made up of bits of mosaic, portrayed our time as one of appalling violence, insensate passion, and gory chaos. Juxtaposed, these eighteen images proved far more moving than they were when read singly, and within the year Hemingway's Imagist art would receive its full due from the critic whose judgment he most highly valued. Meanwhile, however, there was the winter all too slowly becoming spring; there was his family to earn a living for; there were the stories to write, the masterpieces the creation of which was his purpose in life. What to do, how to publish, how to earn both attention and money?

In Ford Madox Ford, the golden walrus, lay Heming-way's solution. 1924 was his most difficult year, a year of actual physical hunger, of hope delayed; yet by its end Hemingway would be well on his way to the American edition of *In Our Time,* to the writing of *The Sun Also Rises,* to the closing months of his close association with the little magazines, to his first meteoric fame. And for that progress Ford Madox Ford was in good measure responsible, for he hired Ernest Hemingway to assist him during most of 1924 in editing his little magazine, *The Transatlantic Review.*

Ford Madox Ford is notoriously not to be trusted for a factual account of the episodes of his picaresque life, but the main outlines of his account — in his memoir *It Was the Nightingale* — of the birth and death of *The Transatlantic Review* are accurate, and most of the details are if not historically factual more colorful than mere history. The history of Ford's *Review* fortunately has been recounted in Bernard J. Poli's excellent recent study, *Ford Madox Ford and the Transatlantic Review,* and thus there exists a sober corrective to Ford's imaginative and entertaining tale.

It begins in the fall of 1923, in Paris. For most of 1923, he had been living in the Ardèche in south-central France at the little mountain resort of St. Agrève with Stella Bowen and their small daughter Julie; there he worked on the first novel in his Tietjens series, *Some Do Not,* until September, when he took Stella and the baby to live in Paris. One of the first people they encountered there was Ford's brother, Oliver Hueffer, whom they bumped into on a traffic island in the Place des Médicis. The result of that meeting was twofold: a cottage back of a dilapidated block of studios in the Boulevard Arago, which Hueffer's wife rented to them for a nominal 200 francs a month; and an introduction to some Paris financiers who had asked Oliver Hueffer to edit for them a periodical in English, no doubt with an ulterior motive in view.

Oliver informed his would-be backers that the man they really needed was his brother, who before the first World War had founded and edited the famous *English Review* from December 1908 until the beginning of 1910. Ford lost his magazine because of his utter and life-long financial incapacity, but not until he had made his reputation, at *The English Review,* as an excellent editor by publishing poems by Thomas Hardy, Henry James's story "The Jolly Corner," H. G. Wells's *Tono-Bungay,* and some early fiction by D. H. Lawrence. The break-up of his marriage at the same time, a break-up both complicated and scandalous, had not helped to set Ford on a steadier path. He had been solaced by Violet Hunt, the first in a succession of solvent, motherly ladies, and like Ford a member of a family that had been prominently associated with the pre-Raphaelite group. Then had come Ford's long service in the first World War, during which he was gassed. Then also, in repudiation of his Teutonic connections, he changed his patronymic of Hueffer to the British surname Ford. After the war and Violet Hunt came Stella Bowen, a young painter from Australia, and four years devoted to farming and raising pigs in Sussex. And now came Paris, bubbling and overflowing, like an immense seething cauldron, with the youthful movements in art and letters — Paris of Dada and the American expatriates, of cubist painters and Imagist poets, of artists' bistros and Diaghilev's ballet. And a part of that Paris was Ford Madox Ford's *Transatlantic Review,* all because of an accidental meeting with Oliver Hueffer, the first since 1916, on a traffic island in the Place des Médicis.

Oliver mentioned to Ford names that were dazzling in the Paris of 1923 and sums that would have made the durability of any journal absolutely certain. But the deal with the French backers fell through. Fortunately John Quinn, benefactor of James Joyce, defender of Margaret Anderson, patron of painters, and a canny corporation lawyer, was in town, and at a reception at Ezra Pound's studio, Quinn met Ford. A few days later, as a result of the meeting, Ford and Quinn founded *The Transatlantic Review,* with Quinn owning fifty-one percent of the shares in it. His secretary, Mrs. Jeanne Foster, carried on most of the negotiations and all the later business correspondence, amid considerable confusion.

By the middle of October 1923, Ford was circularizing his friends and acquaintances to write for his new venture. He was particularly anxious to secure the contributions of his old friends of *English Review* days and wrote Edgar Jepson, Douglas Goldring, H. G. Wells, A. E. Coppard, and others, emphasizing that "though this Review gives me plenty to do and no pay, thank Goodness I've this time no financial responsibility." By November 15 he was telling H. G. Wells that he was rather in a predicament as to an item in the first number of *The Transatlantic Review,* "which ought to be out but has been hung up by impossible printers," White Russians with mere rudiments of English. Conrad, Hardy, and T. S. Eliot all had written notes of "a sort of commendation of the REVIEW as an enterprise," and Ford asked Wells for a similar commendation. Advertisements were coming in: "We have more than paid for the first number by the Paris advertisements alone," he told Wells, and it is true that the advertising in *The Transatlantic Review* was from a surprisingly solid array of such middling to big businesses as Ford's London publisher, Duckworth, the Bank of Montreal, the French Line, and American Express. With that largesse, Ford said hopefully he "ought to be able to buy the moon in the shape of contributions." He ended by assuring Wells that the first number would "be pretty good anyhow — except for the fact that a serial of my own, for motives of economy, takes the place of TONO BUNGAY, it's better than the first number" of *The English Review* — an understandable exaggeration.

Bringing out the first number was rather hectic. Ford had no motive in printing the title without capitals. It was the resultant necessity of a combination of sizes: the size of the front cover, which carried the title, and the size of the thirty-six-point type needed to fill the space planned for the title. Publishing a title in lower case was among the least of the printing problems, for that particular breach of convention was taken for a deliberate display of Communism, and the American Woman's Club of Paris solemnly burned the second number of the *The Transatlantic Review,* alleging that the magazine was not only Communist but indecent, because it published Georges Pillement's story in which one of the scenes transpired in a bathroom.

The misprints made by the Russian printers were to be expected, but their corrections made the pages look like a Soviet battlefield, their procrastination was without parallel. Added to this difficulty were the displays of temperament to which the White Russians at the printer's firm and on the editorial staff itself were given. Probably in November 1923 Ford issued an elaborate announcement-manifesto

to the effect that in his review would be published works of
no national literatures but of Literature, that Paris was the
natural home for such a cosmopolitan venture, and that the
contributors would be those associated with the New Movement (whose names, as he listed them, one recognizes as
associates of Ezra Pound). Also a sample issue was printed
and distributed.

With all this going on, it is hardly surprising to learn
that the first number of the *Review*, dated January 1924, was
several weeks late — but even so it seems to have appeared in
December in England and in January in the United States.
The first issue was not prepossessing. The printers provided a
binding made apparently of toilet paper, and the result was
that later numbers destined for the American trade were ex-
pensively rebound in the United States, a factor that angered
John Quinn to the point of sending many costly cablegrams to
Ford. As a result, the rest of the issues were taken from the
Russian printers and were efficiently printed by Herbert
Clarke, who worked for the British Consulate General.

Such tribulations were overcome by Ford and his sub-
editors. There were so many helpers Ford lost track of their
names; and they all brought out the thirteen monthly numbers of the *Review* from January 1924 through January 1925.
The first was Basil Bunting, "a dark youth with round spec-
tacles, in a large Trilby hat and a blue trench coat with belt."
More importantly there was Ernest Hemingway, who, said the
editor, had been a cowboy before he became a tauromachic
expert; he came to the *Review* shortly after returning to
Paris and meeting Ford about the middle of February 1924.
Indeed it seemed the assistants to the editor "had all been
cowboys so that the office took on an aspect and still more
the sound of a Chicago speakeasy, invaded by young men
from a Wild West show." As Ford's office was a gallery in
a great wine vault on the banks of the Seine on the Île St.
Louis, that the atmosphere was both clandestine and vinous
need not be wondered at. The ground floor was occupied
by William Bird, "thin, bearded, and as nervous as ever";
he had found the space for Ford. In his own office, Bird
operated his big iron seventeenth-century hand press and
stored the books he printed as well as the spare copies of the
Review.

Despite the perils of the five-foot ceiling of the office, it was fine to sit there in that swallow's nest looking across the Seine to the grey houses on the other bank. People came by to purchase a copy of the magazine; "an old, broken London printer" made and served tea in cracked cups; and Ford read his wonderful manuscripts, all of them (he said) except for the few that Mrs. Foster had weeded out in the New York office. Of course if a manuscript were by an obviously illiterate person, not every word need be read; on the other hand, there were the unknown writers who gained acceptance from Ford after he had read the first three lines. In former years such had been the luck of D. H. Lawrence, Norman Douglas, Wyndham Lewis, and H. M. Tomlinson; now, in Hemingway's case, Ford did not read, he said, more than six words before he decided to publish everything Hemingway sent.

On the contrary, Hemingway told Carlos Baker, it was the sub-editor who used to go down to the gallery on the Quai d' Anjou and take a batch of manuscripts outside on the Quai and read them there. He made an annotation of what Ford was to say in refusal; such a note might read, "This stinks but he might write a story if he keeps trying." Without reading the stories, Ford then wrote beautiful letters of encouragement to the rejected contributors. On occasion, Hemingway tried his hand at rewriting the submitted stories; the *Review* even published his parodies of its newsletters in the department of "Chroniques."

Hemingway came to the magazine because of Pound's recommendation. In one of his imaginative reconstructions of the past, Ford recalled seeing them together in Paris, and early one morning a bit later he played tennis with Louis Latapie, Pound, and Hemingway. Then at the reception for John Quinn, on October 12, 1923 (when, actually, Hemingway was in Toronto!), Pound put in a good word for the large-framed young man dancing on his toe points and shadow-boxing with a relic of Ezra's Chinese stage, the rendering in silk of a fat and blinking bonze. Pound said to Ford: "You ought to have had him for your sub-editor," instead of the English conscientious objector who had the job. "He's an experienced journalist. He writes very good verse and he's the finest prose stylist in the world . . . He's disciplined too." Ford agreed to engage the large young man as a

needed aid to the vociferous White Russian Ezra had forced
on the *Review*. "The young man certainly looked disciplined
in a Herculean way. Ezra confirmed my suspicion that he
must have been in the Army. I took him to be one of those
Harrow-Cambridge-General Staff young Englishmen who
make such admirable secretaries until they let you down."
And so it was that Hemingway came to *The Transatlantic
Review*.

After Basil Bunting left Ford's employ, Hemingway was
promoted to the assistant editorship. A "real American secretary," Marjorie Reid (later Mrs. Robert Rodes), was hired;
realistically she demanded a proper salary, and she ran the
office efficiently and brought in the advertisements. The hos-
pitable William Bird not only provided the office space at 29
Quai d' Anjou but helped Ford with technical advice; he
designed the front cover, for example. As his Three Mountains Press did not operate on Thursdays, Ford and Stella
Bowen were able to use the ground floor for Thursday tea, a
frugal tea with biscuits, "after the time-honoured fashion
of editors in Paris." But, admitted the editor of the *Review*,
"you never saw such teas as mine were at first. They would
begin at nine in the morning and last for twelve hours. They
began on Friday and lasted till Saturday. On Sunday disap-
pointed tea drinkers hammered all day on the locked doors.
They were all would-be contributors, all American and nearly
all Middle Westerners. If each of them had bought a copy
of the *Review* we should have made a fortune. Not one did.
They all considered that as would-be contributors they were
entitled to free copies."

The Thursday teas became Friday dances, parties of the
1920's that were the lineal descendants of Ford's parties in
London before the war. Harold Loeb has described blow by
blow and scream by scream the festivities at Ford's rented *rez-
de chaussée*, where Tommy Earp and Wheeler Williams began to fight, where Stella roared: "Miserable man, he's spoil-
ing my party by committing suicide" (an exaggeration, fortunately), and all of a sudden Berenice Abbott fell on her back
in the middle of the floor. Loeb's girl, Lily Lubow, made him
leave, a move he regretted next day when everyone in the
Quarter said it had been a good party.

In their best-known form Ford's parties became dancings

on Saturday nights. As Harold Loeb put it, to spare Stella, Ford stopped giving parties in his home; it was just too much to clean up after them. Instead, he hired a *bal musette,* accordionist and all, for the evening, and invited the crowd in. People bought their own drinks, danced if they liked, and enjoyed the low-life atmosphere. In *A Moveable Feast,* Ford gives Hemingway an invitation: "You and your wife plan to come to the Bal Musette Saturday night. It's quite gay. I'll draw you a map so you can find it. I stumbled on it quite by chance."

"It's under 74 rue Cardinal Lemoine," Hemingway replies. "I lived on the third floor."

Obtusely Ford remarks that "There's no number. But you'll be able to find it if you can find the Place Contrescarpe."

In Chapter III of *The Sun Also Rises,* Jake Barnes is sitting in a restaurant with a *poule* he has picked up, and Mr. and Mrs. Braddocks enter with a party: "Cohn, Frances Clyne, Mrs. Braddocks, several people I did not know" — for whom, read Harold Loeb, Lily Lubow, Stella Bowen, and Ford Madox Ford as Braddocks. Braddocks asks whether Jake is coming to the dancings. " 'And bring your friend,' said Mrs. Braddocks laughing. She was a Canadian and had all their easy social graces." Jake introduces his *poule* as Georgette Leblanc, giving her the name of Margaret Anderson's friend; and they all went their way to the dancing club, "a *bal musette* in the Rue de la Montagne Sainte-Geneviève. Five nights a week the working people of the Pantheon quarter danced there. One night a week it was the dancing-club. On Monday nights it was closed."

Ford wrote that these dances became gradually burdensome and overwhelming, populated not by his friends among the French and British and American artists and writers but by Midwestern state senators in Paris for the night and out for a fling and by American debutantes alcoholically rebelling against Prohibition. At any rate, as editor of *The Transatlantic Review* and model for Braddocks, he did his best for literature and, in print at least, never seems to have resented Hemingway's use of him in *The Sun Also Rises.*

With the end of the Saturday dancings, Ford resumed his Thursday afternoon teas. There could never have been "an artistic atmosphere younger or more pleasurable or more cordial than that which surrounded the *Review* offices and the Thursday teas when they were again instituted," for it was possible now to keep them intimate. William Bird and Ezra Pound came, as did Robert McAlmon and others of the Faithful. "On most Thursdays Mr. Hemingway shadow boxed at Mr. Bird's press, at the files of unsold reviews, and at my nose, shot tree-leopards that twined through the rails of the editorial gallery and told magnificent tales of the boundless prairies of his birth." Ford preferred, actually, Hemingway's stories of his Italian campaign: "They were less familiar." Perhaps the assistant editor of *The Transatlantic Review* glamorized the truth in order to make himself more interesting; he was competing in fast company. Perhaps too that supercilious, comic sketch of "the young man" shadow-boxing on his toe points and amusing his editor by telling tall tales of the boundless American prairies caused the Old Man, in *A Moveable Feast,* to sketch the now-dead editor as an ignoble presence to be trusted neither for truth nor cleanliness.

Not all was play at the *Review.* The simple tasks Ford describes Hemingway performing included his trying to insert as a serial the complete works of the Baronin Elsa von Freytag-Loringhoven. The editor generally turned round in time to take them out of the contents table. When he paid his month's visit to New York in June-July 1924, however, Hemingway took charge and accomplished his purpose at the expense of cutting a short story by Mrs. H. G. Wells down to forty lines and the "London Letter" down to three. It is a good tale, none the worse because neither Catherine Wells's story nor the "London Letter" appeared in the September *Review*

Hemingway really was much busier than Ford implied. Not only did he help with the editorial chores, he actually ran the *Review* for two issues while the editor was in America; he acted as a scout for Ford, securing some unlikely American contributors (his reporter friend Guy Hickok, Ring Lardner, and Donald Ogden Stewart) and some of his Parisian friends (Gertrude Stein, Ralph Cheever Dunning, and Evan Shipman) as well as the mad Baroness; and he contributed editorial matter, letters, and some of his best fiction.

The two men worked well together because they had to; nevertheless on many points there was neither agreement nor mutual trust between them. As evidence, Gertrude Stein recalled that Ford once said of Hemingway, "He comes and sits at my feet and praises me. It makes me nervous." At fifty-one Ford was old enough to be Hemingway's father. The older man had his antecedents in the British gentry and the German nobility as well as in the bohemian Victorians of the pre-Raphaelite group. He had gravitated to the raffish side of bohemia, had lived through a good many ups and downs, and in 1924 was, though hampered by his financial ineptitude, reaching the apex of his long career. In contrast, Hemingway was just starting as a writer. His background was solidly bourgeois, his people the businessmen, doctors, and ministers of a prosperous Chicago suburb. His antecedents were as piously Protestant as Ford's were piously Catholic. Like Ford, he was in full rebellion against their restrictions, but where Ford became a freethinker, Hemingway became a Catholic.

What, then, did they have in common? Devotion to writing as a sacred craft, most obviously. They also shared the trauma of service in the first World War; if Ford's period of war service was longer, it was no more intense and no more scarring than Hemingway's. The masterpieces both men created directly involved the debacle of the first World War and were written and published during the 1920's. In 1923 Hemingway started *in our time* and Ford *Some Do Not,* the first of his Tietjens series about the war. Then came Hemingway's *The Sun Also Rises* in 1926 and his *Farewell to Arms* in 1929; the Tietjens series continued with *No More Parades* in 1925 and *A Man Could Stand Up* in 1926, and concluded with *The Last Post* in 1928. Editor and sub-editor shared, further, a compulsion to write idealized autobiography: Hemingway composed his Nick Adams stories, *The Green Hills of Africa,* and *A Moveable Feast,* and Ford wrote *Thus to Revisit, Return to Yesterday,* and *It Was the Nightingale.* To their mutual misfortune, both Ernest Hemingway and Ford Madox Ford became figures of legend long before they died, and disentangling the legend from the history of their lives is difficult, even impossible at some points.

There is still another similarity. Precisely because, in

their different ways, both men rebelled against what Shaw's
Alfred Doolittle called middle-class morality, they abandoned
something at the root of their respective native traditions.
Instead, they assimilated themselves to the international tradition. True, they did so with ambivalence about what they
were doing, yet their action was deliberate and definitive for
their art. Ford regarded himself as *the* novelist who in the
postwar generation still carried onward the torch lit by Henry
James and Joseph Conrad. More ambiguously, Hemingway
spoke of Mark Twain's *Huckleberry Finn* as having informed
his own fiction and also spoke of the influence of Stephen
Crane's war stories; in the same passage in *The Green Hills
of Africa,* he also paid tribute to Henry James: "The good
writers are Henry James, Stephen Crane, and Mark Twain.
That's not the order they're good in. There is no order for
good writers." And in the memorial supplement to the October 1924 issue of *The Transatlantic Review,* Hemingway said
in his essay, "Joseph Conrad," that he had read Conrad's
novels early and was unable to reread them, but "from
nothing else that I have read have I gotten what every book
of Conrad has given me." Both men came together and
worked side by side on the *Review* because of a mutual need.
Beyond that need lay their differences, major differences to
be sure; beyond those differences, however, lay a measure of
agreement important to consider, for it embraced not only
the New Movement but the international tradition that the
title of *The Transatlantic Review* exemplified.

In its first number for January 1924, the *Review* mani-
fested its twin commitments. The emblem of the magazine
appeared on the front cover: in a circle, a ship breasting a
high wave, and at the top of the circle, "Fluctuat." Ford
Madox Ford explained the emblem as symbolic of the birth of
The Transatlantic Review amid turmoil and of its tumultuous
if sometimes gay career: "Foreseeing this, we took for its crest
the ship that forms the arms of the city of Paris and, for
its motto, the first word of that city's device: 'Fluctuat . . . .'
'It is borne up and down on the waves.' Had its career been
prolonged we had intended to add the rest of the device: 'Nec
mergitur' — 'and does not sink.' . . . It was not to be."

The commitment of the *Review* to the New Movement
was made clear by the lead piece, E. E. Cummings's "Four

Poems"; Ford liked Cummings's work so much that he had accepted the entire group as soon as he had read no further than the first ten lines of one of the poems. From prewar days there appeared A. E. Coppard with his story "Pelagea" and a reprinting of a story, "The Nature of a Crime," jointly by Joseph Conrad and F. M. Hueffer. Jean Cassou represented the young French contingent with "Concorde," an experimental set of reflections on the ever-pressing subject of peace; Robert McAlmon represented the young expatriates with his story "Elsie"; and D. Chaucer — a favorite *nom de plume* Ford used ("D." was for "Daniel")— began his monthly lucubrations on literature with an essay entitled "Stock Taking." The pre-Raphaelite past received its tribute from Luke Ionides, an acquaintance of the Pounds, with his first installment of "Memories" (he died before the year was out but not before completing his memoirs for the magazine).

There were letters for the occasion from H. G. Wells and T. S. Eliot. Wells was brief and complimentary; Eliot was aggressive and discursive. "Personally," he asserted, "I have always maintained what appears to be one of your capital tenets: that the standards of literature should be international. And personally, I am, as you know, an old-fashioned Tory. We are so far in accord." Eliot went on to say that the present age, "a singularly stupid one, is the age of a mistaken nationalism and of an equally mistaken and artificial internationalism." He called for national literatures that complemented, not contradicted, the other national literatures: "Let us not have an indiscriminate mongrel mixture of socialist internationals, or of capitalistic cosmopolitans, but a harmony of different functions. But the more contact, the more free exchange, between the small number of intelligent people of every race or nation, the more likelihood of a general contribution to what we call Literature." On the other hand, Eliot explained himself as opposed to another vehicle for the younger writers as an unnecessary discrimination in favor of youth. America already had too many such periodicals, and England did not seem to have any younger writers anyway — a judgment in which Ford heartily concurred. A review, said Eliot, is not measured by the number of stars and scoops it gets. "Good literature is produced by a few queer people in

odd corners; the use of a review is not to force talent but to
create a favorable atmosphere." Ford would best serve that
purpose if he published the work of writers of whatever age
who were too good and too independent to have found other
publishers. That at any rate was what Eliot's own quarterly
The Criterion had attempted: "to find good work which
either could not appear elsewhere at all, or would not appear
elsewhere to such advantage." Eliot was agreeing with the
policy set by Scofield Thayer and James Sibley Watson, Jr.,
for *The Dial* when he concluded with a request that Ford's
Review "give us either what we can support or what is worth
our trouble to attack. There is little of either in existence."
Such a trenchant statement as Eliot's was worth any number
of prospectuses, and certainly Ford tried to make his *Review*
live up to that exhortation.

Besides the contributions in the front section of the *Review,* Ford planned two other features. One was the exten-
sive department called "Chroniques," a compendium of newsletters from his correspondents in America (a feature usually
entitled "And from the United States"), in England (the
"London Letter"), the new Irish Free State ("Litir o Éirinn"),
and of course France (the French letter was invariably in
French); correspondents occasionally popped up in more
exotic places as well, as when Hemingway sent in his "Pamplona Letter."

The second additional feature was the monthly supplement to the *Review.* The second number, for February 1924,
was devoted to Music, the third, for March, was devoted to
Art, and the fourth, for April, was devoted to Letters; there
were thus three series of quarterly supplements planned.
George Antheil's Sonata 3 was reproduced in part in the February supplement, along with Ezra Pound's sketch of the
composer, William Atheling's "Notes for Performers" (with
marginalia by Antheil), and Dynely Hussey's "Music in London: the 'Novelties' of the Autumn Season." The March art
supplement had articles in English and French accompanied
by reproductions of pictures by Georges Braque, Gwen John,
Man Ray, Cedric Morris, and Pound's friend Louis Latapie.
The supplements were lavish, well printed, well planned, and
executed with the *brio* that called forth H. G. Wells's praise of

Ford as "one of the greatest poets and one of the greatest
Editors alive."

It was in the April supplement, the first to be devoted
to literature, that Hemingway made his appearance in *The
Transatlantic Review* as a contributor. By this time, moreover, he was having a discernible effect on the magazine
editorially; in the front of the number appeared contributions by Gertrude Stein and Djuna Barnes, two writers whose
work he especially liked. Djuna Barnes's story "Aller et
Retour" may well have been solicited by Hemingway — not
all his preferences were for what Ford condescendingly if
amiably termed the Middle Western, or cowboy, school of
writing — and Gertrude Stein's "The Making of Americans"
was certainly printed because he scouted it for the *Review*.
Like the loss of his suitcaseful of manuscripts, the publication of *The Making of Americans* became one of the episodes
in the Hemingway legend as well as one of the best-known
episodes of the 1920's.

First, Gertrude Stein's side of the story, as she tells it in
The Autobiography of Alice B. Toklas. She had known Ford
ever since those prewar days when he lived with Violet Hunt;
in 1924 she was aware he was in Paris, and she had seen
copies of *The Transatlantic Review,* which she found interesting but had thought nothing further about. One afternoon
Hemingway came to her house very excited about Ford Madox Ford and the *Review.* He told Gertrude Stein that Ford
wanted something of hers for the next number and that he,
Hemingway, wanted *The Making of Americans* to be serialized in it; he must have the first fifty pages at once. Gertrude
Stein was of course quite overcome with excitement at the
idea, but there was no copy of the manuscript except the one
that Alice Toklas and she had bound. "That makes no difference," said Hemingway, "I will copy it." Whereupon
Miss Toklas and he did copy the manuscript, and it was
printed in the April number of *The Transatlantic Review.*
"So for the first time a piece of the monumental work which
was the beginning," wrote Gertrude Stein, "really the beginning of modern writing was printed," and later on when
things were difficult between Hemingway and herself, she
always remembered with gratitude that after all it was Hemingway who first caused to be printed a piece of *The Making*

of Americans. ("A piece," indeed! The thing ran on interminably, and was killed off only when the *Review* itself died.
But back to Gertrude Stein's yarn.) As Alice B. Toklas, Gertrude Stein reported Gertrude Stein as always saying, "Yes sure
I have a weakness for Hemingway. After all he was the first
of the young men to knock at my door and he did make Ford
print the first piece of The Making of Americans." As Alice
B. Toklas, Gertrude Stein begged to differ: "I myself have
not so much confidence that Hemingway did do this. I have
never known what the story is but I have always been certain
that there was some other story behind it all. That is the way
I feel about it."

Still in character as Alice B. Toklas, Gertrude Stein went
on to say that Hemingway had done it all. He copied the
manuscript and corrected the proof. ("Correcting proofs,"
mused Alice B. Toklas, "is like dusting, you learn the values
of the thing as no reading suffices to teach it to you.") So
in correcting these proofs, "Hemingway learned a great deal
and he admired all that he learned." It was she, he said to
Gertrude Stein, "who had done the work in writing The Making of Americans and he and all his had but to devote their
lives to seeing that it was published." Published it was, as a
book, by Robert McAlmon's Contact Editions; but that is
another story.

The context of Gertrude Stein's acknowledgment is,
however, rather more bitter than sweet, being ten remarkably frank pages about Ernest Hemingway as man and writer,
in the course of which occurs the famous passage in which she
reported Sherwood Anderson and herself as being endlessly
amusing on the subject of "their good pupil" who was "yellow." "He is," she insisted, "just like the flat-boat men on
the Mississippi River as described by Mark Twain." And why
was he a good pupil? He took training, and anybody who
takes training is a favorite pupil. "You see," Gertrude Stein
explained, "He is like Derain. You remember Monsieur de
Tuille said, when I did not understand why Derain was having the success he was having that it was because he looks like
a modern and he smells of the museums." But what a story,
she added, that of the real Hem, and one he should tell himself but alas he never would. After all, as he himself mur-
mured, there is the career, the career.

Hemingway's account, in *A Moveable Feast,* is considerably more reserved than is Gertrude Stein's but would be both more damaging and more convincing because of its balance and qualifications — would be, that is, were he telling the whole of his story. After paying tribute to her discovery of many truths and rhythms and the uses of words in repetition, Hemingway remarks that Gertrude Stein disliked the drudgery of revision and the obligation to make her writing intelligible, although her *amour propre* demanded publication and official acceptance, especially for her incredibly lengthy novel called *The Making of Americans.* The chronicle of an American family, this book began magnificently, as Hemingway admitted, and continued on very well with long passages of dazzling competence — but then the author still continued her story, repeating herself without end. A more active artistic conscience, a more carefully exercised writer's energy would have thrown these repetitions into the wastebasket. Hemingway asserted that Ford Madox Ford was forced by him to publish *The Making of Americans* serially in *The Transatlantic Review* while realizing that the chronicle would outrun the life of the *Review* itself. The sub-editor's penance for his generosity was both immediate and prolonged: he had to read all the proof for Gertrude Stein, as she disliked such a chore. And with that, Hemingway rested his case.

That Hemingway's case is not the whole truth about the episode is shown by the letters to Gertrude Stein collected in Donald Gallup's anthology of letters to her, *The Flowers of Friendship.* Shortly after Hemingway had met Ford and had become his assistant on the *Review,* he wrote Gertrude Stein, on February 17, 1924, telling her that Ford was delighted with her stuff and intended to call. Hemingway said he had told the editor that there were six volumes of *The Making of Americans* and that the *Review* would print the first installment in the April number, where of course it duly appeared. Hemingway then talked about the rate of payment to contributors, thirty francs per printed page, and advised Gertrude Stein not to be too haughty and to take the offer. But, he warned, Ford would never be able to pay nine thousand times thirty francs; despite the remarkable scoop Ford had obtained only through Hemingway's energetically obtaining genius, there was, the sub-editor inferred, a limit to

the enthusiasm of his editor. One is struck by the tone of the
letter, a close imitating of Pound's own scouting for his pro-
tegés. The difference, of course, lay in the fact that Pound
was an older and a widely recognized writer and that Hemingway at twenty-five was advising the much more experienced
Miss Stein on her relations with editors.

When John Quinn died in June, there arose the primary
question as to whether Gertrude Stein's long fiction would
be printed, for *The Transatlantic Review* itself might fold.
Jane Heap stepped into the breach and had a talk with Viscountess Rothermere, then the patron of Eliot's *Criterion*.
Jane told Gertrude Stein that she had talked to Lady Rothermere and if the *Review* failed, "we" (presumably the Viscountess and herself) were going to arrange to have Gertrude's "novel" transferred to *The Criterion* and there to continue its serialization. As Gertrude Stein was a stockholder
in Ford's *Review*, matters must have been serious indeed.

Hemingway also stepped in. He scouted a backer for
Ford, purely on the basis that the *Review* printed *The Making
of Americans* and was edited by old Ford, who as a veteran
of the war must not be allowed to go haywire. Hemingway
wrote persuasively that Gertrude Stein must leave her manuscript with him, that even though the monthly *Review* ended,
Ford might pull off the feat of starting a quarterly journal,
which would continue to serialize *The Making of Americans* — and that, in any case, as Eliot was no friend of Gertrude
Stein, it was out of the question that *The Criterion* would
publish her book. Jane's drag would not be strong enough to
make Lady Rothermere force a fight on that question.

Such were the finances of the *Review* that Ford was not
able to pay Gertrude Stein the thirty francs per page he owed
her. He apologized to her in a letter of September 18 for having delayed her check and went on to say that when Hemingway had first handed over her manuscript, he had given
his editor the impression that *The Making of Americans* was
a long short story that would run for about three numbers —
a reference to the fifty pages of the work Hemingway had requested for the *Review*, for the first installment. Ford continued: "Had I known that it was to be a long novel I should
have delayed publishing it until my own serial had run out"
— a reference to *Some Do Not* — "and then should have of-

fered you a lump sum as serials are not accounted so valuable as shorter matter. I do not get paid for my own serial at all, neither does Pound for his." Ford then mentioned Hemingway's report of an offer of "real money" by *The Criterion* for *The Making of Americans* and advised Gertrude Stein that since her book consisted of three or four novels, to let them have the second novel and rook them all she could. He was never one to stand in a contributor's way. But the alleged offer by *The Criterion* proved a false alarm, as Hemingway had predicted, and Ford, whatever he may really have wished, continued to serialize the work. Perhaps nobody really wished to publish *The Making of Americans*. That Ford did serialize it was due to Hemingway's persuasive powers.

Examining the same opposing stories and the same series of letters, Bernard Poli comes to the conclusion that "it is clear that in this negotiation Hemingway played false to everybody," but the opposite may be true. In *A Moveable Feast* Hemingway admittedly pretends to no historical accuracy, and his account of his scouting *The Making of Americans* is so summary as to be a fragment. His correspondence with Gertrude Stein fails to show premeditated duplicity, though it does display eager partisanship for her and a rather snide attitude toward Ford. But neither Gertrude Stein nor Ernest Hemingway was the irritant agent in this episode. Ford himself was to blame — not for fraudulence of intent, not for any meanness of heart, but for sheer muddleheadedness. He could no more keep straight his relations with his friends, his wife and mistresses, his editors and contributors than he could his business accounts. Stella Bowen herself, who of all people should have had the most intimate insight into Ford's affairs in 1924, wrote that the early days of *The Transatlantic Review,* before it became apparent that by no conceivable chance could it be made to pay, were great fun: "The whole thing was run in conditions of the utmost confusion. Everything that could possibly go wrong with regard to the printing, paper, packing, forwarding and distribution did go wrong." This situation exemplifies Ford's muddle. It seems likely that, persuaded by Hemingway's enthusiasm and told the truth about the length of *The Making of Americans,* Ford decided to take a chance on it; perhaps he did not fully realize just how long it was from Hemingway's partisan sketch.

Then, too, it may be that threatening the ongoing publication of the work was Ford's way of attempting to attract more money from Miss Stein, who had bought some shares in his *Review*; its discontinuance would mean the discontinuance of her serial. When a new backer for the *Review* was found by Hemingway, Ford still attempted to get out from under his bargain with Miss Stein by pleading that Hemingway had given the wrong impression about the length of *The Making of Americans* — surely not an efficient or businesslike editorial attitude to take. From beginning to end, Hemingway's story is consistent. In October 1924, he asked Gertrude Stein whether she had received Ford's letter about the alleged misunderstanding. He accurately recited Ford's allegations and called them lies.

In still another respect that April 1924 *Transatlantic Review* was important to Hemingway's advancing career and to his developing art as a writer. The literary supplement appended to the issue published his untitled story, the third piece in the supplement, indicated merely by "III." The placing of this story was a great compliment; the general heading for the creative writing in the supplement was "From Work in Progress," and the first example of such work was James Joyce's untitled portion of what eventually turned out to be *Finnegan's Wake,* the initial publication of any part of it. The second piece of work in progress was Tristan Tzara's "Monsieur A. l' antiphilosophe," and then came the Hemingway story. In the American edition of *In Our Time* it was the first story in the collection, appearing just after the first vignette. The order was especially appropriate, for the vignette was the first of those printed in *The Little Review,* and similarly "Indian Camp" was the first of the Nick Adams stories to be published.

The setting of "Indian Camp" is Hemingway's remembered family summer vacation country of northern Michigan with its lakes, forests, lumber camps, and Indian settlements. Nick is a young boy at the outset of adolescence. His father, a doctor, is called out of bed one night to be rowed across the lake to the nearby Indian camp in order to attend an Indian woman in labor. Without an anaesthetic and with only the minimum of surgical equipment, things he carries wrapped in a handkerchief, the doctor performs a successful

Caesarian operation. Nick must hold a pan of water during the operation and must listen to the woman's incesssant screaming. When he complains, his father says that there is no anaesthetic, "But her screams are not important. I don't hear them because they are not important." They are important, however, to the Indian woman's husband. Having cut his foot with an axe three days before, he has been lying in the upper bunk of their one-room shanty, unable to get away from the sound of his wife suffering in the bunk beneath his. When the doctor starts to congratulate "the proud father" of the new baby, he suddenly finds out that the Indian, unable to bear what his wife has been going through, has taken a razor and has cut his throat from ear to ear. And then begin Nick's questions: "Do ladies always have such a hard time having babies?" "Why did he kill himself, Daddy?" "Do many men kill themselves, Daddy?" "Is dying hard, Daddy?" Leaving the scene, the doctor gives only the most banal and reassuring answers, and sitting in the stern of the homeward-bound boat with his father rowing, Nick feels quite sure that he would never die.

The story is shocking, or to put the matter in another way, tremendously moving. Its effectiveness lies in Hemingway's manipulation of style and matter, in his relating the most violent and bloody action in a laconic, almost stolid style. Nouns and verbs in simple constructions bear the burden of the work. The incidents are rigorously selected; because Hemingway is reticent about the goriness of the birth and sparing in his description of the suicide, he manages all the more strongly to shock his readers into a realization of the meanings behind the action. The dialogue is set down without comment, as though it had been recorded. Of course it had not, and of course Hemingway creates the effect of verisimilitude through deliberate artifice, but the effect is the thing here, and he achieves it superbly. Nick is innocence learning about the pitfalls of adult life, and at the end the banal lies with which his father answers the boy's probing questions deceive him — but the reader, a wiser man, knows that Nick will one day be undeceived. One of the subtlest effects in "Indian Camp" is Hemingway's juxtaposition of the primitive, who is all feeling and intuition, and the civilized man, who is all efficiency and scientific impartiality. To the emotional, bloody squalor of the primitive is opposed the Olympian problem-solving of the civilized man. But the civilized man refuses to answer truthfully the boy's questions, and the primitive cannot. The doctor's cloud of words is, effectively, as mystifying as the primitive's inability to communicate. Both ways of life are not only incomplete in their extreme opposition but are stultifying. Both lead Nick to a choice; but that choice of course exists outside the framework of "Indian Camp." Not until the final story of *In Our Time,* "Big Two-Hearted River," does Nick Adams choose. On another level of meaning, the story holds a reader's interest, for the theme of suicide runs morbidly and consistently through Hemingway's life as well as through his art. Harry Morgan of *To Have and Have Not,* Robert Jordan of *For Whom the Bell Tolls,* Colonel Cantwell of *Across the River and into the Trees* if not suicides in the narrowest sense wilfully choose death as against living on terms not theirs; and in 1928 Dr. Clarence Hemingway, fatally ill of diabetes and complications, shot himself. His widow mailed Ernest Hemingway the pistol with which his father had made an end of things; and Hemingway, ill and dying, shot himself while cleaning one of his guns at his hunting lodge in Ketchum, Idaho, on July 3, 1961.

The story moves along in a balance of juxtaposed figures. Instead of asides and explanations put by the author, the juxtapositions themselves furnish the comment. In sum, Hemingway was applying his Imagist technique — refined during the composition of his poems and the vignettes of *in our time* — to the problems of prose fiction. Reading "Indian Camp" in the context of the early 1920's, as it appeared in *The Transatlantic Review,* grouped with the experimental prose of James Joyce and Tristan Tzara, one savors the shock of recognition — recognition of an astonishing, novel talent. Ezra Pound's apparently casual words to Ford Madox Ford were not, after all, the good-natured exaggerations of a professional promoter but rather were the astute prophecy of a brother artist: "he's the finest prose stylist in the world."

Pound's judgment of his protegé was borne out explicitly in the final review printed in the April literary supplement. By "M. R.," as the office secretary Marjorie Reid signed herself, this untitled review of *in our time* may well be the earliest notice Hemingway's pamphlet received. The high praise is bestowed without reservation: " 'Here ends the inquest into the state of contemporary English prose, as edited by Ezra Pound and printed at the Three Mountains Press.' [This was a reference to the fact that the series of publications that *in our time* concluded had been limited in number by the general editor, Pound.] This brief comment is affixed to the sixth and last volume in a series of six selected by the editor as most indicative of the present trend in English literary expression. In eighteen chapters the longest of which measures scarcely two pages Mr. Hemingway gives pictures of life in the army, in Italy, in the bull rings of Spain, in the gardens of the King of Greece. He projects the moments when life is condensed and clean-cut and significant, presenting them in minute narratives that eliminate every useless word. Each tale is much longer than the measure of its lines." It is disappointing that Marjorie Reid failed to discern the basic distinction between Hemingway's vignettes and conventional prose fiction — or even unconventional prose fiction, for that matter. Here were images, not stories; "Indian Camp" was the kind of story that resulted when Hemingway applied his technique to fiction. M. R. went on to quote from "chapters" she especially admired, to exemplify her general praise of the book. For example, of Chapter VI, she said that Hemingway gives "the sort of detached circumstances that always penetrate deep into the consciousness in the wake of a bald and imperious fact," and of Chapter IV, more sensitively and more nearly in accord with the author's intention, she said of this, "the shortest in the book," that it "contains only eight lines but it leaves a vivid impression of the scene that took place 'in a garden in Mons.' "

At about the same time, back in Oak Park, Illinois, Hemingway's parents had a very different reaction to *in our time*. They had ordered six copies of the Paris edition but had been shocked and horrified at some of the contents, especially the tenth vignette (which was not one of those *The Little Review* had printed and was excluded from the American edition). As Hemingway's elder sister remembered the incident, her father "was so incensed that a son of his would so far forget his Christian training that he could use the subject matter and vulgar expressions this book contained that he

wrapped and returned all six copies" he had ordered from
William Bird. When Mrs. Hemingway remonstrated about
sending all the copies back to the Three Mountains Press,
Dr. Hemingway declared that he would not tolerate such
filth in his home.

Hemingway's admirers had to be found outside his family,
but they did exist. Of the April number of *The Transatlantic
Review,* a correspondent from Assisi writing in the July number and signing himself as "Old Glory" (it was Pound) said:
"April number good. Especially Hem. and Djuna. Want
more of them and of McAlmon and Mary Butts [a British
contributor in the expatriate group]. May number not so
good . . . Best action you have is in McAlmon, Hemingway,
Mary B., Djuna, [Alexandre] *Cingria* [a music critic], K.
Jewett [a very youthful critic and reviewer for the maga-
zine]." Through the support of these enthusiastic champions,
the cause and name of Ernest Hemingway were being advanced in *The Transatlantic Review* number by number.

The May issue of the *Review* placed Hemingway's next
contribution, his newsletter entitled "And to the United
States," in the department of gossip and news, "Chroniques."
It was an exile's reply to the usual American Letter headed
"And from the United States," and like similar pieces in the
magazine it is a mélange of gossip and opinion. The reversed
direction indicated in the title of the letter also indicates a
reversal of intention; this is not seriously intended but instead is another of Hemingway's burlesques. As so often
was the case in his relationship with Ford and the *Review,*
Hemingway poked fun at the intentions and the deeds of
the vanguard. Calling on his experience of journalism for
"And to the United States," he wrote up the doings of the
expatriates caught up in the New Movement as though he
were a society or a shipboard-news reporter, so that the letter
becomes a parody of a social news column in make-up and
style.

Dated "The Quarter. Early Spring," its sixteen separate items range in length from one sentence to a paragraph
of half a page. Attacking *The Dial,* its award, and "the critics," for whom Hemingway entertained a lively and life-long
aversion, the first and longest item of the sixteen begins with
the complaint that "for every writer produced in America

there are produced eleven critics. Now that the *Dial* prize had gone to a critic" — a reference to the bestowal of the award for 1923 on Van Wyck Brooks in January 1924 — "the ration may be expected to increase to 1/55 or over. As I have always regarded critics as the eunuchs of literature . . . But there is no use finishing that sentence. If this letter is accepted that means one hundred and fifty francs which relieves one of that responsibility to follow through which is imposed in golf and creative writing." One metaphor from sports led to another, which enforces his point and also marks the second time Hemingway publicized a relationship as lively and long-lived as his regard for critics: bullfighting. (The second vignette *The Little Review* printed had been his previous mention of the sport.) "Did you, however, ever see a bull which had withstood the bad sticking of the matador, led off to the corrals by three thin steers? And did you ever see a bull who had earned the president's reprieve to the corrals, and after, of course, to the abattoir, dully refuse to follow the steers and insist on being killed in the ring? And then did you watch the terror of the trained steers and their angular attempts to jump out of the ring over the barriers?" Readers familiar with Hemingway need not be told the significance of the bull and the steers.

The rest of the newsletter consists of vignettes, brittle small pieces of gossip important now because they reveal whom Hemingway knew, whom he associated with, and whom he would have liked to know; because they reveal prejudices already formed, some of which are as indicative of the future as his remarks about critics and steers; and also because they reveal his growing familiarity with the expatriate life that constitutes the raw material of *The Sun Also Rises*. The second item reads in part: "as for America, Henry Strater has just gone there. New York gets a good painter and the newly opened *Boxing Montparnasse* in the rue de la Gaieté loses a needed supporter." Added to the critics and bullfighting, another preoccupation emerges: Hemingway's involvement with boxing. The tenth item adverts to the same topic. Of a French boxer, Hemingway wrote that "Mr. Criqui, of Belleville, in the contemplation of whose work I experience a certain ecstasy which is not given me by reading the works of my contemporaries, will make his re-appearance some day

early in the Buffalo Stadium. Mr. Siki who can do nothing
without giving me a certain measure of enjoyment writes of
his projected return from Cuba where, unhappily, he suffered
a serious fall from a hotel window." Much of this is panache,
another brick in the edifice of the Hemingway legend; but
it does show where Hemingway learned the back-ground for
such early stories as "Fifty Grand." Similarly, Item 13 reveals
Hemingway's interest in racing, the background of another
of his stories of the Paris years, "My Old Man": "Epinard,
the race-horse, is reported by Mr. Sparrow Robertson the
sporting writer, to be fit and well. Mr. [Harold] Stearns, the
sportsman and critic [and former managing editor of *The
Dial*, who earned his living as the tipster for the Paris edition
of the *Herald Tribune*], who was reassured by the writer that
Sir Galahad, the racehorse would not win the Lincolnshire
says that he bears no hard feelings." Two other items, the
fourteenth and fifteenth, relate to bullfighting: "The *tem-
porada* was inaugurated in Barcelona by the Messrs. Chicuelo
[the "kid" of the bullfighting episode Margaret Anderson
published], Salanda and Villalta. Mr. Salanda returned to the
infirmary before the conclusion of the afternoon, turning over
his work to Mr. Villalta. There were 28,000 spectators"; and
"Since seeing his first bull-fight, Mr. William Bird, the publisher, no longer finds it necessary to read the cabled base-
ball reports from New York." Provincial New York! The
final item relates to Hemingway's self-advertised *gourman-
dise*: "Oysters will continue to be eaten until after the Grande
Semaine despite there being no -r- in either Mai or Juin.
There are certain advantages in living in the same latitude
as Labrador."

There were also certain advantages in displaying oneself
as a man of the world, a man well acquainted with Gertrude
Stein and her Picassos (thirty of the best in the world, no
less — an item the author admitted should really be published
in the *Financial Tips* column), Djuna Barnes (who, according to Item 7 and her publishers, "is that legendary person-
ality that has dominated the intellectual night-life of Europe
for a century"; she was in town, and although Hemingway
had "never met her, nor read her books . . . she looks very
nice"), and the writer himself — that is, if Item 9 be trusted:
"Mr. Antheil, the composer, pianist, and, with Mr. Pound,

student of harmony, has taken up drawing in a sketch book. He has already completed sketches of Mr. Stravinsky, Mr. Diederichs and various instruments of the orchestra and has in contemplation sketches of Miss Beach, Mr. McAlmon and the writer." Juxtaposed and seen in proper perspective, the sixteen items compose a bright, hard mosaic portrait of a time and place — and of a writer. Even the 150 francs Hemingway named as the price of his contribution play their part in the total composition. They indicate the very modest sums Ford paid his contributors; they also say, in their context, that such gossip is journalism and so worth doing for an explicit reason, the check for 150 francs this particular contributor received. The implicit reason for writing "And to the United States" is more interesting, however; Hemingway wrote it to define his persona, the image of himself he was constructing, in its way as much a work of art as any novel. Every item of the sixteen in the newsletter thus counted toward the accomplishment of the writer's career or of his fiction. Bullfighting, the Spanish scene, the life of the expatriates, Paris, the sporting scene with its racing and boxing, the Quarter, the circle of artists and composers and poets from many lands, the life of art dominated by such figures as Igor Stravinsky, Ezra Pound, Gertrude Stein, Pablo Picasso, all counted in the formulation of the writer and in the composition of his work.

Ford Madox Ford's "Editorial" began the "Chroniques" for the August 1924 number. It was given this importance because Ford announced that he must leave the *Review* temporarily: "We are journeying Westwards, leaving the helm of the review — on a ship one thinks of helms — for the time being in the hands of Mr. Ernest Hemingway whose tastes march more with our own than those of most other men. There may have been editors who, from the inwards of their chairs, could survey mankind from China to Peru: we can not. So from the decks of the good ship — let us say Ville Lumière [an allusion to the emblem of the magazine] — we continue our speculations as to what may be the matter with England." Ford did as he said he would and went on with his monthly analysis of British affairs, one of the few dull features of an otherwise attractive journal; and he ended with a curious editorial directive that in a later issue he had to explain away. "Articles about subjects . . . . do not happen to be much our affair," he concluded, but *The Transatlantic Review* for August 1924 might "call itself a relatively serious number" because, in the English taste, it had essays by several distinguished essayists: "Mr. etc. . . Hemingway continue . . ."

When Ford returned from his journey, he explained in the editorial matter of the magazine for its September issue "the mysterious words *Mr. etc Hemingway continue . . .*" with which the July "London Letter" (an error: he meant the July "Editorial") concluded: "We had asked Mr. Hemingway to make some concluding notes on this and other matters at the end of our Letter and made these jottings to remind him. Our jottings were misunderstood: hence that cypher." That is to say, Ford had asked Hemingway to write editorially on the way "the Young of to-day" regarded Joseph Conrad and had failed to leave sufficiently explicit instructions; hence the mystifying phrase.

Two points here need to be examined. First, whither "Westwards" did Ford travel, and why? Second, how did Hemingway discharge his duties as acting editor of Ford's magazine, for example, did he write any editorial matter for the August issue as Ford directed? Answering these questions demands some explanation, by way of preface, of the finances of the *Review*.

The Transatlantic Review depended on the largesse of two men, John Quinn and Ford Madox Ford. Quinn put up 51% of the funds, about $4,000, and owned 51% of the company stock. Ford found the rest of the money and owned some of the rest of the stock in the parent company. Besides himself and Quinn, he recalled four shareholders: Miss Natalie Barney, Miss Gertrude Stein, the Duchesse de Clermont-Tonnerre, and "a lady whose name I cannot call to mind"; each of these owned a certificate for a thousand francs. As so often, Ford must be corrected; by November 1924, his shareholders, besides himself and John Quinn's estate, included Stella Bowen, Nancy Cunard, Natalie Barney, Mrs. Romaine Brooks, William C. Bullitt, Marjorie Reid's fiancé Robert Rodes, William Bird, Ezra Pound, Gertrude Stein, and Mr. and Mrs. Krebs Friend, two backers Hemingway introduced into this circle. As for the money needed for operating the magazine, Ford supplemented Quinn's bounty with the proceeds of his own literary labors. He did a good deal of hack work for other, more solvent journals and poured into the *Review* the sums thus earned. That he tried to pay most of his contributors his dealings with Gertrude Stein and Ernest Hemingway exemplify; but he did not pay himself for his serialization of *Some Do Not,* which he concluded before the novel itself concluded, giving as his reason that the book version had been issued in England by his publisher Duckworth. Nor, one rests assured, did Ford pay himself for his writing as Daniel Chaucer and for his editorials and newsletters; and of course he not only earned no salary as editor but instead went into the hole each month in order to continue operating the magazine. Whatever Ezra Pound contributed was in the way of a gift, as Ford informed Gertrude Stein. And there must have been other equally generous contributors; after all, nobody among the contributors to *The Little Review* received payment, and most of the little magazines then as now were published on the same principle. *The Dial* was in a class by itself in its perennial solvency, a state admired and envied and, inevitably, complained about.

John Quinn's generosity to Ford is much carped at in *It Was the Nightingale.* Quinn's terms, Quinn's peremptory manners, Quinn's legal quibbles, even Quinn's health receive their querulous due in Ford's memoir. But, as he had to admit, when Quinn died, "That was the end of the *transatlantic review.*"

About a month before Quinn died, he ordered Ford to come to New York in order that they might discuss problems relating to the 800 copies of the *Review* sent on to New York each month for distribution by the publishing firm of Thomas Seltzer. Seltzer was not paying for the copies sold; the French were not buying the *Review*; and besides Quinn's bounty, Ford's personal subsidy, and the advertising, only Duckworth, the British distributor, kept the magazine afloat with regular payments for the copies he sold. The trip was useless, perhaps worse than useless: Ford was saddled with the expense of the voyage and his New York bills; Seltzer settled nothing (except the arrangements for publishing *Some Do Not* in October 1924); and Quinn, then in his last days, was unable to keep the appointment that Ford had come all the way to New York for. He returned to Paris, from where, on July 29,

at the Quai d' Anjou, one finds him commiserating with
James Joyce, just operated on for trouble with his eyes, and
confiding to Joyce that the news of their benefactor was
"about as bad as can be." As the editor himself suspected
by now, he was fighting a losing struggle to continue the publication of his magazine, and his main effort to that end was
to keep *The Transatlantic Review* going for a complete
volume of twelve monthly issues.

Ford's bad luck was, however, Hemingway's good fortune. True, Hemingway then as years later regarded the
Review with very mixed feelings; in 1951 he told Carlos
Baker that his post as sub-editor was a real *corvée,* forced labor
without visible recompense. Yet the sub-editorship enabled
Hemingway to associate with one of the great literary editors
and novelists of the day on an intimate, professional basis, it
furnished the kind of social-literary entrée even Pound had
not been able to give, it granted an opportunity to learn from
the inside what his own generation was attempting to write,
it enabled him to publicize himself in everyday association
with men like James Joyce and Ezra Pound, and finally it
opened to him the pages of a journal sympathetic to his stories and essays. The last factor is perhaps the most important,
for along with the arguments of Sherwood Anderson and
Harold Loeb, Marjorie Reid's review of *in our time*, Hemingway's status as sub-editor, his publication of editorial matter and newsletters, and his three Nick Adams stories —
"Indian Camp," "The Doctor and the Doctor's Wife," and
"Cross-Country Snow" — must have worked together to persuade Horace Liveright to bring out the American edition
of *In Our Time* in 1925. Given his head by Ford, how did
Hemingway discharge his duties? The two issues of *The
Transatlantic Review* pertinent here are those for August and
September 1924. The first of these he must have worked on
during June, for the famous trip to Pamplona occurred in
early July. During late July, after the return from Pamplona,
Hemingway edited the September issue of the *Review.* Hemingway thus was not in charge of *The Transatlantic Review*
for long periods of time, and of the two issues Ford charged
him with, that for August was in large part the editor's
handiwork.

Hemingway's acting editorship consisted of arranging

further the contents for which he had not been primarily responsible; writing editorial matter as directed to do by Ford (but, in the event, with Hemingway's own satirical prejudices in evidence); and, finally, in printing the work of several acquaintances whom Ford, at most, tolerated. On one surprising occasion, he went with Marjorie Reid as the guest of honor at a dinner of leading authors and was there acclaimed; looking back on that evening, she told Bernard Poli she thought her companion added luster to the *Review* "or maybe it did to him!"

In "Chroniques" for the August number, Hemingway wrote the usual American Letter, this time entitled as usual "And out of America." Although unsigned, the newsletter is ascribable to him on the score of style, thought, and subject; it displays another of Hemingway's antipathies that went counter to those of the editor — an opposition to Dada and particularly to that fountainhead of Dada, Tristan Tzara. Perhaps to lend weight to his own remarks, Hemingway in arranging the "Chroniques" for the issue preceded his own editorial remarks with André Salmon's essay, "État de la poésie française," a brief survey of the convalescent state of French postwar poetry in the course of which Salmon wrote: "one will see, to be concise, that, in our days, Dada itself reopens tombs in order to select masters from them." This was the piece that inspired Hemingway, not Ford's request to write about what the young people of today thought of Joseph Conrad.

"We had written a long editorial," began the acting editor. It had been all about Jean Cocteau — two of whose contributions, solicited of course by Ford, appeared in the literary supplement to the issue! — "who does not, we believe, know English, translating Romeo and Juliet, and the snobbism of language in general, and how pleasant it is to appear to know, to really know, languages other than our own and how difficult it is to do so, and what profound admiration we have for Americans who really do know French and how tired we get of others who pretend to and how very much better dadas the American dadas, who do not know they are dadas, unless, of course, Mr. Seldes has told them, are than the French and the Roumanians who know it so well — and so on — and it all seemed very dull and not worth writing." The needed relief came when "Mr. Don Stewart whom Mr. Tzara cannot read in the original, and we feel sure has not yet read in translation, brought up I. Gaspari by Ring Lardner."

Hemingway then acknowledged permission to publish: the magazine was "indebted primarily to Mr. Lardner, secondarily to Mr. Stewart, and in the tertiary stage to Mr. Ben Hecht who borrowed it from Mr. Stewart to copy and then printed it in the Chicago Literary Times from which we reprint it." That Hemingway then knew Ben Hecht, the editor of *The Chicago Literary Times,* is probable, and as an *aficionado* of little magazines and as a former Chicago journalist he may well have been aware of this latest addition to *Poetry* and *The Little Review.* Hecht put out his short-lived and uproarious journal from Chicago in 1923-24; its distinctive differences from most little magazines were its format, which was that of a newspaper, and its raucous sense of humor. While Hecht did print work by vanguard writers like Maxwell Bodenheim and Samuel Putnam, he was not interested in experimental writing except as it was also writing that shocked because of subject or treatment of subject. Like many a newspaperman, Hecht loved a spoof, and *The Chicago Literary Times* went in for spoofs such as "I. Gaspari" just as it went in for such headlines as "On the Terrifying Art of Being a Real Woman." Hemingway's attitude toward *The Transatlantic Review* had a good deal in common with Hecht's toward the little magazines and the groups that published them and wrote for them; perhaps this partly accounts for the harsh words about French and Roumanian Dadaists.

Donald Ogden Stewart, probably the agent through whom Hemingway procured "I. Gaspari," first appeared in *The Transatlantic Review* in the literary supplement to the July issue; the supplement included "Fragments from Work in Progress," and Stewart's contribution, "Fragment IV" (footnoted as "From John Brown's Body; A novel"), was a burlesque, like the two "Fragments" by Jean Cocteau (one of Hemingway's aversions) that immediately preceded it. Stewart's satirical comment on college fraternity life, old grads, and the cult of football is the slick, clever product of a writer who knew these things as only a Skull and Bones man could know them. Far from being a member of Pound's circle of expatriates, and a contributor to the little magazines,

Stewart was one of those Midwestern humorists like George Ade and Ring Lardner, who wrote for large popular audiences. He not only condescended to Hemingway's friends but told him he ought to see more of "people who mattered."

Hemingway first met Don Stewart in Europe in 1923 and saw a great deal of him in 1924 and 1925; in August 1924 their names were linked together in news stories about their prowess as amateurs of bullfighting. Hemingway, another Midwestern humorist, must have been aware of Stewart's *Parody Outline of History,* a great success in 1921 because it burlesqued H. G. Wells's *Outline of History.* In 1922 Stewart burlesqued Emily Post's book of etiquette in his *Perfect Behavior*; and his *Mr. and Mrs. Haddock Abroad* in 1924 took advantage of the new wave of American tourism to Europe. Charles Fenton says that Hemingway much admired *Mr. and Mrs. Haddock Abroad* and adds that one of the last pieces of journalism Hemingway attempted at this time was a humorous account of bullfighting that Stewart rejected in 1924 for *Vanity Fair.* They nevertheless remained on good terms; Stewart tried, again unsuccessfully, to sell the manuscript of *In Our Time* to Doubleday Doran and sent Hemingway a big Christmas check by way of consolation. Uncharacteristically, Stewart contributed a second story, to the December *Transatlantic Review,* which contained his "Morning of Mrs. Gordon Smythe," a satirical portrait of an old matron ill at ease in a French hotel. In thus bringing another popular humorist to Ford's readers, Hemingway was imposing his own canons on the magazine, canons in some respects very different from his editor's.

As for "I. Gaspari," Hemingway concluded his prefatory remarks to the playlet by expressing as his only regret that "Mr. Tzara will be unable to read it. But there may, ultimately, be a translation. By that time though Mr. Tzara will probably be too busy on a translation of Marlowe or some other Elizabethan for next year's Cigale to bother." In his biography of Ring Lardner, Donald Elder describes Hemingway's editorial as being by Ford ("by the editor") and as commending "I. Gaspari" to the attention of André Breton, "hinting that Ring was doing what the Dadaists and the surrealists were trying to do, and doing it much better." Hemingway's blunt language is hardly a hint; and Tzara not Breton is the target. While "Surrealists" as a term was already in use at the end of 1922, according to Matthew Josephson, the movement was not officially established until 1924, and even an insider like Hemingway may not have been aware of it, inasmuch as he linked Cocteau and Tzara together as Dadaists.

"I. Gaspari" followed Hemingway's remarks; one of Lardner's familiar skits, it seems to be a burlesque of Pirandello (one guesses) and superficially resembles a Dada theatrical happening mostly in its inconsequence. Fundamentally, Dada had little enough in common with the wit of Lardner and the Midwestern humorists; for, fundamentally, his comedy is "intelligible," its flights are only apparently inconsequential and actually proceed by patterns of association of thought and imagery. Like the writing of Gertrude Stein, Dada was not intended to be intelligible, it was intended to be thoroughly inconsequential and not to make sense. Only as nonsense — if one may be pardoned the paradox — did either Dada or Gertrude Stein make sense, only, that is to say, as a kind of purely visual or purely aural patterning quite arbitrary in its demands, quite different in its dependence on associational impulses (and these different from those depended upon by Ring Lardner). Ernest Hemingway's protest that Gertrude disliked the drudgery of revision and the obligation to make her writing intelligible indicates that *au fond* he did not sympathize with her experiments and almost certainly did not understand what she strove for. Much the same is indicated with regard to his attitude toward Dada.

Ford had yoked Joyce and Hemingway with Tzara in the April literary supplement, an arbitrary editorial act that Hemingway inferentially denied by his attack on Tzara and on Dada, in the next issue. His antipathy for both Dada and Tzara was indicated clearly enough by Item 5 of his burlesque gossip column in the May number of *The Transatlantic Review*: "Dada is dead although Tzara still cuddles its emaciated little corpse to his breast and croons a Roumanian folk-song, written by Princess Bibesco, while he tries to get the dead little lips to take sustenance from his monocle." But this can best be dismissed as a crude personal attack on a man Hemingway disliked. In no detail does it indicate Hemingway as being aware of what Dada was about. Tzara's witty adoption of that appendage of the aristocracy and the upper middle class, the monocle, in order to *épater les bourgeois,* only *épaté*ed Hemingway, who misunderstood Tzara's reason for wearing it.

Dada was an attack on the decadence of modern Western culture profounder and more far-ranging than any ever made by Hemingway, for all his bleak theology of *nada.* In his memoir of the 1920's, *Life among the Surrealists,* Matthew Josephson says that Dada was truly an international phenomenon, for it was initiated in Switzerland in 1916 by Tristan Tzara and a group of pacifists, then taken up in Germany with great enthusiasm in 1918, and at last taken up in France. Hugo Ball, one of its earliest advocates declared that Dada opposed bourgeois logic as the author of modern war and chaos: "Dada is a great clownery. Since the age aims at the destruction of all that is noblest and best in life, the Dadaist courts the absurd, loves every kind of disguise, game or deception. The Dadaist fights against the agony of the times and the intoxication of death." And in his early manifestoes. Tzara wrote, "Let each man proclaim: there is a great negative work of destruction to be accomplished. We must sweep everything away and sweep clean." At the end of 1919, a French literary group of Tzara's sympathizers invited him to come to Paris to organize demonstrations such as had shocked the burghers of Zurich. There in the Café Voltaire, Tzara and his cohorts had sung and danced about like bears or waddled around in gunny sacks before a public constantly astounded by such antics, insulted by the Dadaists as "stinking bourgeois," and nevertheless always on hand as paying customers to receive more of the same treatment.

The Paris Dadaists included André Breton (who broke away and founded Surrealism in 1924), Louis Aragon (who became French Communism's chief literary ornament in later years) , Philippe Soupault, Georges Ribémont-Dessaignes, and Jacques Baron, then only seventeen. Their plays, to which Hemingway referred in his editorial note, were notorious for aggressive nonsense and for the riots they caused, the climactic brawl occurring in the spring of 1923 between the factions of Tristan Tzara and André Breton, when Tzara's play, *Le Coeur à gaz,* was produced in a Paris theater. The violence, the alienation, the disorientation of Dada was a response to the values of a world that wrought the chaos and

destruction and senselessness of the first World War. The
very name itself meant nothing. Tristan Tzara was said to
have found the title for the cult by opening a big dictionary
at random.

At bottom Hemingway was opposed to the sweeping de-
structiveness of Dada; he was far too traditional in attitude.
In "Riparto d'Assalto," the vignettes published in *The Little
Review*, and "Indian Camp," he asserted a sardonic pessimism,
but his vision was no bleaker than Mark Twain's, for like
Mark Twain he still sought to communicate, he somehow
still saw art as a positive resource, he still wished to come
to terms with the bourgeois world and to make his success
according to its standards. Despite the wit of Dada, its vision
was a darker one than Hemingway's.

His attacks upon Dada and upon its founder and chief
exponent were never directly answered. Tzara did take note
of Hemingway's references to his theatrical activities and to
Jean Cocteau's translation of *Romeo and Juliet*; but in this
riposte printed in the October number of *The Transatlantic
Review*, Tzara refused to lock horns with his opponent and
merely took note of the editorial inaccuracy regarding his
translation of Marlowe's *Faustus*. Hemingway had sneered
that Tzara would not be able to read Ring Lardner's "I.
Gaspari" and that although Lardner's burlesque might ultimately be translated, by that time Tzara would probably be too
busy on a translation of Marlowe or some other Elizabethan
to bother reading it. Writing in French, Tzara politely informed *The Transatlantic Review* that its editorial note had
been slightly inexact. He was working on an adaptation of
Faustus in collaboration with Nancy Cunard; also a contributor to the *Review*, she was notoriously one of the Brightest
Young People of the decade and the rebellious daughter of
the famous London hostess Lady Emerald Cunard (*née*
Maude Burke of San Francisco). The rest of Tzara's letter to
the editor concerned the problems of attempting to transpose
into French the quality and the intensity of Marlowe's work,
and only the final sentence obliquely commented on Hemingway's remark about "the snobbism of language in general,
and how pleasant it is to appear to know, to really know,
languages other than our own and how difficult it is to do
so." Addressing Ford, Tzara said that the editor of the *Review*

knew better than he the difficulties one had in translating the
sense of a phrase, of retaining its original value, that power
of words which is developed unequally in two tongues as different as English and French. Tzara's letter was remarkably
temperate — he was noted for having wrestled André Breton
all over the stage of the theater during the premiere of *Le
Coeur à gaz* — and his moderation probably was due to Ford's
having published his work in the *Review*. Since the editorial
introducing "I. Gaspari" as much better Dada than French
Dada was anonymous, Tzara probably believed that the attack
was Ford's work and that it called for a mild answer. Privately
Ford may have explained that the editorial was Hemingway's,
for Tzara continued to publish in the *Review*. Perhaps as
an amends — and a rebuke to Hemingway — seven of Tzara's
poems appeared in the December issue, in which Hemingway's story "The Doctor and the Doctor's Wife" also appeared.

That the editor and his sub-editor were at cross-pur-
poses becomes increasingly obvious when one takes a close
look at the September 1924 number of *The Transatlantic
Review*. The contents of the front pages opened with three
poems by Bryher, the pen name of Robert McAlmon's new
wife, Winifred Ellerman. Then came two poems by the Baronin Elsa von Freytag-Loringhoven, followed by Dorothy
Richardson's story, "In the Garden," Nathan Asch's story,
"Marc Kranz," John Dos Passos' story, "July," and Guy
Hickok's sketch, "Herriot in the States," ending with the
month's installment of Gertrude Stein's *The Making of Americans*. Of these seven writers, at least four were introduced
into the issue by Hemingway: the Baroness, Hickok, Gertrude
Stein, and Nathan Asch. Ford had already made it clear
that he would not print the writing of the Baroness. Attired
in a brassiere made of "milktins connected by dog chains,"
she had used his name as a reference at the British Consulate
General in an unsuccessful attempt to procure a *permis de
séjour*, and as a result of this imbroglio the British Embassy
discontinued its subscription to the *Review*. As for Gertrude
Stein, Ford had done his best to work off *The Making of
Americans* onto *The Little Review* or *The Criterion*, and he
had taken it in the first place only because Hemingway persuaded him to. Guy Hickok was, in a way, less suitable even
than the Baroness; his account of Edouard Herriot's tour of

the United States in 1924 is good journalism, freshly and crisply written, but journalism all the same and out of place in a little magazine of the vanguard.

The fourth writer whom Hemingway placed in the September issue of *The Transatlantic Review,* Nathan Asch, was published for the first time anywhere, with his autobiographical short story, "The Voice of the Office," which appeared in the June issue. Also autobiographical was his story in the September issue, "Marc Kranz," about a young man who escapes from his New York office and goes to Paris. In 1961, Asch told Bernard Poli that Hemingway had said it was he who first found Asch's work: "His story was that one morning as he was about to go to the W. C., he picked up some mss. from Ford's desk, and he said he got so excited about my story, he forgot to button up his pants." Asch later met Ford and learned of the acceptance of the story. To the twenty-two year-old Asch, acceptance meant a great deal, but his gratitude was vitiated by the fact that Ford was not easy to be with. There was something unnatural about the mixing of generations, a kind of mortal rivalry, and Asch realized then how impatient Hemingway felt when he had to show the least mark of deference to Ford. As regards Asch's debt to Ernest Hemingway, Harold Loeb recalled that Asch had shown his stories to Loeb, then helping to finance another little magazine, *Broom;* he liked the stories but not enough to offer to send them to *Broom.* Afterward Asch took them to Hemingway, who, said Loeb, had already acquired a reputation as a stylist although he had completed only a handful of short stories: "Ernest read Nathan's work carefully and sat down with him and went over the stories carefully paragraph by paragraph. I was surprised not that Hemingway's comments were helpful, but that he was so eager to help."

Still another writer, John Dos Passos, may have had his story "July" placed in the September issue by Hemingway, even though Hemingway had not scouted it for the *Review.* They had been acquainted since the end of 1918, but, as Dos Passos wrote in his memoir, *The Best Times,* it was not until 1924, "when Hem, as most of us called him, and Hadley were living at the sawmill on rue Nôtre Dame des Champs that we began to play any part in each others' lives. . . . *In Our Time* was out" in the Paris edition, "and I was trumpeting it abroad." Unlike his friend, Dos Passos greatly admired Ford, and when the editor of *The Transatlantic Review* asked him for a story to publish in the *Review*, Dos Passos went to considerable trouble to fish out "July" and rewrite it.

Excluded from the issue were the usual installment of Luke Ionides' memoir, the usual criticism by D. Chaucer, and the usual fiction or memoir by Ford Madox Ford, whose sole contribution was an American Letter, "And from the United States," in the "Chroniques" department. In his newsletter Ford discussed obliquely Hemingway's changes in policy. "And from the United States" was based on his recent trip to New York, but the editor used the occasion to comment on what he entitled "An Americanization." "During our absence on those other pavements" of New York, his *Review* had, he said, "been ably edited by Mr. Ernest Hemingway, the admirable Young American prose writer. Except for the London Musical Chronicle of Mr. Hussey" — Dyneley Hussey, Ford's good friend — "and the charming letter on music in America which we ourselves procured from Miss Malkiel of New York, the present number is entirely of Mr. Hemingway's getting together." Ford guessed that the number must prove an agreeable change for his readers, provided as they thus were "with an unusually large sample of the work of that Young America whose claims we have so insistently — but not with such efficiency — forced upon our readers. It should thus please our esteemed correspondent Old Glory," i. e., Ezra Pound. The editor pointed out that Dorothy Richardson, Eric Satie (who had contributed to the rear pages, under "Communications," the "Cahiers d'un mammifère"), and Mary Butts (who, as a matter of fact, did *not* contribute to the issue!) were English or French but that otherwise the contributors were American "by birth, marriage, adoption, or in such ways as show American predilections sufficiently strong to let them form part of the embattled minority of the western world." And he added his good wishes: "May they help to hoist the flag of U. S. Art a little higher on the National flagstaff."

Despite the breach between the editor and his sub-editor, occasioned by Hemingway's high-handed ways with the Baroness, his publication of writing by his cronies, and his insulting references to such valued contributors as Jean Cocteau and

Tristan Tzara, Ford's American Letter thus does not make
explicit a disagreement between his assistant and himself. To
the contrary, his "And from the United States" reveals his
usual generosity toward younger writers and his admitted
partiality for the new American writing. Commenting on
this writing in *It Was the Nightingale,* he spoke of the Midwest of the 1920's as seething with literary impetus. Eighty
per cent of the manuscripts in English he reviewed for his
Review "came from west of Altoona," and of these, forty per
cent were of such a level of excellence that one might just
as well close one's eyes and select one at random as try to
choose between them. Attempt as Ford did to divide the space
of the *Review* into equal portions devoted to French, English,
and American writing, the preponderating share of its pages
went to the Midwest. Certainly with the contributions of
Jean Cassou, Georges Pillement, Georges Ribémont-Dessaignes, Philippe Soupault, and their group, *The Transatlantic Review* managed to print a good deal of new French writing, but all the same, partly through "the patriotic coercion
of Mr. Hemingway," the *Review* was Midwestern by more
than half and French by slightly less than a third; the remaining sixth, consisting mostly of newsletters, came from "the
Eastern States, New York, and England," though few manuscripts came from England. The influence of Hemingway
on the contents of *The Transatlantic Review* was second in
importance only to that of the editor himself.

CHAPTER 5

"YOU want something about Pamplona, because it is such a lovely name to have in the review. I should write it: I owe it to you because I published X . . . in the review. And I said, 'Well I don't look at it that way,' and came home," to the apartment over the sawmill at 113 rue Notre-Dame-des-Champs. This suggestion of an apology for having published the verses of Elsa von Freytag-Loringhoven begins Hemingway's honorable amends for implementing his disagreement with the editor of *The Transatlantic Review* over the Baroness's poems ("Novemberday" and "Enchantment") in the September number. The apology took the form of the "Pamplona Letter" that appeared in the *Review* for October 1924, as Hemingway made clear: "Now are we square about X? If not, remember that you yourself printed W., and more honour to the review, although many a lousy magazine had done it, and I challenge you to write to W. and ask him if the two poems by X . . . weren't good."

The "Pamplona Letter" was not a casual undertaking but stemmed from Hemingway's enduring fascination with Spain in general and specifically with the art of bullfighting.

At the end of 1921, Hadley and Ernest Hemingway had dis-
embarked at Vigo, the port famous for sardine and tuna fishing, in Galicia. From their brief stay there, Hemingway sent
back his first European news story to the *Toronto Star Weekly,*
where it was published on February 18, 1922. "Tuna Fishing in Spain" is a brief account but one obviously written *con
amore,* and interesting not only in itself but also as the earliest
foreshadowing of *The Old Man and the Sea* in its preoccupation with the brown-skinned fishermen pursuing the great
fish in Vigo Bay, "shouldering out of the water like porpoises
as they herd the sardines, then leaping in a towering jump
that is as clean and beautiful as the first leap of a well-hooked
rainbow." Landing one "is a back-sickening, sinew-straining,
man-sized job even with a rod that looks like a hoe-handle."
But landing a big tuna "after a six-hour fight," fighting "him
man against fish when your muscles are nauseated with the
unceasing strain," and finally bringing him up alongside the
boat, "green-blue and silver in the lazy ocean," purified a man
and enabled him to "enter unabashed into the presence of
the very elder gods," who make such a fisherman welcome.

In 1922 Hemingway first spent a portion of a summer in
Spain, and the next year he returned there for the Pamplona
feria held in the first two weeks of July. Out of these experiences came further news stories for the *Star Weekly*: "Bull
Fighting — It's a Tragedy," in the issue of October 20, 1923,
the story in which the Gin Bottle King from Chicago appears;
"Pamplona in July," in the *Star Weekly* a week later, October
27, a brilliant if straightforwardly conventional account of
the fair and its concomitant "World's Series of bull fighting";
and least importantly, "Trout Fishing in Europe," in the
Star Weekly for November 17, 1923, in which Spain received
only passing mention. After the loss of his manuscripts almost
the first writing Hemingway composed was a description of
the young matador Chicuelo, as recounted by the Gin Bottle
King, one of the six vignettes *The Little Review* published
in its Exiles number. This date in the spring of 1923 shows
that as early as the summer of 1922 Hemingway had become
enamored of the *corrida.* The vivid vignettes of the bull
ring in *in our time* showed further that Spain and bullfighting and the complex of cultural values summed up in the

wonderful nightmare of the Pamplona *feria* were becoming decisive in directing Hemingway's growth as an artist.

Now, on his third trip to see the bullfights and attend the fair, it would seem that writing about the annual running of the young bulls to the *corrida* in Pamplona might prove a congenial task for Hemingway, but neither time nor mood was propitious. It was difficult to concentrate while "a cousin" pulled film he had taken out of a flat tin can and held it up against the light and said: "This is where the regular matadors are in eh?" and "Did the picador get badly hurt?" and "I'd like to see this run off." And Hemingway tried to write (and actually did write) and commented, "We ought to have a spool," while Pamplona — all the overwhelming reality of its impact upon his sensibility — got further and further away.

It would be gone in a little while if one talked about it or saw many more of the pictures on the roll of film: "Photographing kills anything, any good thing, just as it improves a bad thing i. e. the faces of movie stars." He had taken his typewriter into another room in an effort to compose his letter, but the effort was futile: "Can you see how much I do not want to write it?" It could only be journalism anyway because he did not understand it any more than Don Stewart did; and when one wrote journalism, he preferred to be well paid for the job. That was the only reason for writing journalism; when one destroyed the valuable things he possessed by writing about them, he wanted big money for doing so. Once one puts a thing into words, "unless you do it 'on your knees,' you kill it. If you do write it 'on your knees' (I forget who said that about knees and it may have been somebody very banal), the thirty francs a page is only a supplementary reward." Those words were written despite three interruptions; writing in his hotel room was difficult. It was easy to write with interruptions in a newspaper office, but it lacked conviction for readers: "It is only by never writing the way I write in a newspaper office, though, that I make you believe I can write." The difference in purpose dictated the instrument used, the pencil was exchanged for the Corona, because Hemingway was writing journalism rather than the stories that he could make his readers believe in, in which he could make his readers believe he could write. In addition Ford's rate of payment, thirty francs per printed page, was no great incentive to inspire one's talent.

In a supreme effort to rise above journalism and to write as it were on his knees, he then typed out four paragraphs, two of them of but one sentence each, sketches in the best manner of *in our time*, limning the running of the bulls of the Pamplona *feria* from their *corrales* chasing "the younger element of Pamplona" through the streets of the town into the bull ring. But the effort was exhausting and unrewarding: "Really I can't write anything more. It's no good. Either it would bore a lot of people or else next year Cooks would be running tours down there. The less publicity it has the better. Practically all the people that deserved to be at Pamplona were there this year" — at which the editor inserted a hurt *"Merci!"* Hemingway went on to say he realized that many right-thinking Anglo-Saxons opposed any glorification of his favorite sport; and he promised to get those of the deserving who had not been at the Pamplona fair in 1924 "down next year by private means; not a public appeal. We are not missionaries. Nor appreciators. Nor exhibitionists. The more people that think it is a terrible, brutal degrading relic of etc. the better." Within the next few months one of his stories about bullfighting would be refused because it told about such a terrible, brutal, degrading relic of etc., and his uncompromising admiration for the matador's art and courage inevitably proved to limit his appeal.

The quasimystical attraction for Hemingway bullfighting held he expressed in quoting the words of Pablo Picasso, who also had made the trip to Pamplona for the fair: "As Picasso said to Don Stewart. 'You know it's absolutely the only thing left in the world. Bul [*sic*] fighting that is.' Don was demonstrating his busted ribs," gained in the caper that had made newspaper pictures and headlines in America and Canada. And Hemingway added prophetically, though he could not make the remark in foreknowledge of *A Moveable Feast*: "For the rest of it, the amateur fights, etc., the consciousness of what happened is plenty. It is only when you can no longer believe in your own exploits that you write your memoirs." He ended his "Pamplona Letter" with the promise to give Ford the first bullfighting story he wrote, a promise he could never fulfill because of the cessation of *The*

Transatlantic Review: "If after about four more San Firmins I ever get so I can write anything worth a hoot about it you shall have it as you should naturally have it in any event. Until then let us write letters on unpleasant things where you have nothing to lose: oike and the Quarter."

By the time Hemingway's "Pamplona Letter" appeared in the *Review*, his Pamplona exploits had gained him more publicity than all his poetry, fiction, reportage, and self-advertising gossip put together. He had gone with Hadley and his new friends Robert McAlmon, John Dos Passos, and Donald Ogden Stewart to Pamplona for the fair and the 1924 World's Series of bullfighting. The mystique of the sport must have been enhanced by repeated potions of Fundador brandy, and the result was another news story, this time not by but about Ernest Hemingway. The *Toronto Star* used the United Press account of the doings in Pamplona, dated from Paris, July 30, 1924, accompanied by a photograph of both the Hemingways. The *Chicago Tribune* carried a story substantially the same but dated from Madrid, July 28, and excited and pleased about the figure his son was making, Dr. Hemingway supplied the *Tribune* with a picture of Hemingway taken in Milan during December 1918.

The *Tribune* gallantly omitted Hadley Hemingway from its story and reported that "Stewart, Hemingway, John Dos Passos and Robert McAlmon, all American writers resident of Paris," had gone to Pamplona "to take part in an old fashioned celebration" in which the custom was "to barricade the side streets of the town and drive the bulls for the day's fighting from the station to the arena, the larger part of the populace flying before them. Afterwards a bull with bandaged horns is sent to the arena, where the toreadors play leap frog and tag with the animal":

> Part of the initiation of young manhood in Pamplona consists of being thrown by the bandaged bull. Stewart and Hemingway participated successfully the first day. But on the second day Stewart was thrown. He had said he could leap on the bull's back, blow smoke in his eyes, and then beat him down. The chief toreador presented Stewart with a scarlet cloak, which the American could not refuse. Then during the handshaking the bull

rushed for Stewart, lifted him on his horns, tossed
him over, threw him into the air, and later tried to
horn him. Hemingway rushed to rescue his com-
rade and was also gored. He was saved from death
only because the bull's horns were bandaged.

Donald Ogden Stewart survived with two broken ribs, Hemingway with some bruises. When Stewart demonstrated the
honorable proofs of his prowess, well might Pablo Picasso
remark that bullfighting was absolutely the only thing left in
the world. For Hemingway the man-to-bull encounter was,
in those days just after the event, more than could be set
down, the consciousness of what happened was plenty, and
only when he could no longer believe in his Pamplona exploits could he set them down in his memoirs. But he never
did. Instead he awaited another summer, another *feria*, in
1925, and put it all into Chapters XIII-XIX of *The Sun
Also Rises*. What survived in *The Transatlantic Review* were
the stunned impressions, the bright shards of images, the awkward attempts to explain why journalism could not con-
vincingly convey the intense reality of the Pamplona fair.

Death in the Afternoon, Hemingway's collection of stories and handbook to the art of bullfighting of 1932, explains
in more explicit detail his response to those early Spanish
experiences that the "Pamplona Letter" in its more disjointed
way refers to. The tone of one well-known passage is remi-
niscent and thus perhaps enforces a formulation upon the
discrete, separate experiences of the early 1920's that they
did not possess, a formulation related to the artistic unity
of *The Sun Also Rises* rather than to the Imagist vignettes,
the surrealist shards of the "Pamplona Letter." As so often
in his writing about his art, Hemingway made, in the passage
from *Death in the Afternoon*, a sharp distinction between
his journalism and his fiction.

Trying to write fiction in the early 1920's, Hemingway
found (so he recalled) the greatest difficulty was putting
down what really happened in action (aside, that is, from
knowing and writing what one truly felt rather than what
one conventionally was supposed to feel and had been taught
to feel). What were the actual things that produced the emotion one experienced? "In writing for a newspaper you told
what happened and, with one trick and another, you com-

municated the emotion aided by the element of timeliness which gives a certain emotion to any account of something that has happened on that day." Capturing as it were the essence of an event was an achievement not so easy to attain, for the real thing (did Hemingway's phrase consciously echo Henry James's irony?), "the sequence of motion and fact which made the emotion and which would be as valid in a year or in ten years or, with luck and if you stated it purely enough, always," this was beyond one's straining grasp; yet Hemingway was working very hard to achieve such a sequence of motion and fact. He found his solution in Spain. The only place where one could see life and death, "i. e., violent death now that the wars were over," was in the bullring, and thus he wanted very much to go to Spain, where he could study the violent confrontation of life and death stripped to essential terms. He was, he repeated, trying to learn to write, commencing with the simplest things, "and one of the simplest things of all and the most fundamental is violent death."

What Hemingway was trying to do, as one commentator, Richard P. Adams, has described the attempt, was to store or freeze the kinetic energy of action by means of the artistic techniques of writing, "so that it could be released again in the readers as the same kind of motion or kinetic energy that it was" in the author himself and in the life he observed and lived. If Hemingway succeeded in this aim, continued Adams, he would achieve a kind of immortality not only for life in general, but in some degree for himself individually. To illustrate the point Adams turned to another comment Hemingway made on bullfighting, in *Death in the Afternoon*. The essence of the greatest emotional appeal of bullfighting, maintained Hemingway, is the feeling of immortality that the bullfighter feels in the middle of a great arena and that he gives to the spectators: "He is performing a work of art and he is playing with death, bringing it closer, closer, closer to himself, a death that you know is in the horns because you have the canvas-covered bodies of the horses on the sand to prove it." The matador emanates the feeling — the aura — of his immortality, and the enthralled spectator begins to share the mana put out by the bullfighter. "Then, when it belongs to both of you, he proves it with the sword."

As Richard Adams explains, in Hemingway's writing the

technical means of bottling up the motion he wants his readers to feel — of securing their complete empathy — is often
precisely this kind of playing with death, this deliberate approach, as close as can be made, to violent extinction: "The
violence serves not only to emphasize the reality of the motion, but to provide a sort of containing field of force by
means of which the motion can be held and preserved until
the reader gets around to releasing it." The advantage the
writer holds over the matador, Adams contends, is that his
effects may not be as intensely immediate but can be made
to last much longer: "The bullfighter's immortality is of
the moment; the writer's, with luck, forever."

In *The Transatlantic Review* one searches in vain for
any such fully formulated aesthetic response as Hemingway
described in *Death in the Afternoon* and Richard Adams
elaborated on in his critique. The first story to exploit
Hemingway's discovery of a further range where gleamed the
epiphanies of Joyce above the metaphors of Imagism is "The
Undefeated," published in 1925; to be sure, the "Pamplona
Letter" adumbrates this story, but even that connection one
discerns by hindsight. Yet Ford Madox Ford and his journal
remain of unique importance in the saga of Hemingway's
Paris years, for in *The Transatlantic Review* Hemingway saw
his experiments on the printed page, month after month.
There is no surrogate for regular publication.

The "Pamplona Letter" deeply impressed Ford Madox
Ford; as "Ed." he appended a paragraph in French to the
effect that a writer's metier was a veritable dog's life. Nobody
in the world understood what one wished to say or what one
gave in effort, blood, sweat, stated the writer of this dour
advice, who concluded that an artist would never find in his
entire life a single soul to tell him whether at the end he
is the world's greatest genius or the world's lowest creature.
The point to make about Ford's implied advice is perhaps not
that he intended to discourage Hemingway, whose utter dedication was to writing as a sacred calling that he practiced "on
his knees," nor that the French quotation was intended to
show Hemingway what a hard vocation it was he had chosen
(a fact he already was aware of from current experience), but
that the editor of *The Transatlantic Review* took with complete seriousness Hemingway's courageous attempt to set

down on paper, to communicate, what at the time remained an incommunicable experience. Like James Joyce's, Hemingway's method was the creating of an epiphany. The word was used by Joyce in the special sense that has since become famous, but essentially it refers to the communication of meaning by means of a verbal image. Yet the meaning conveyed through these verbal means is paradoxically paraverbal, by its intensity transcending anything mere words can say. Familiar as he was with such theories and attitudes then current, Ford not only recognized Hemingway's difficulty but, as a brother craftsman, empathized with him.

Although editor and sub-editor were by now at odds, that October number of *The Transatlantic Review* outwardly marked the climax of Hemingway's connection with Ford Madox Ford's magazine. Besides the "Pamplona Letter" with the editor's appended comment, there also appeared two other items that show his importance to the *Review*. One is Tristan Tzara's correction of Hemingway's unsigned editorial contrasting the humor of American writers, as exemplified by Ring Lardner's "I. Gaspari," with the Dadas both French and Roumanian. The other is a brief memorial tribute, "Joseph Conrad," in the special supplement for the October issue.

After Conrad's death on August 3, Ford organized a memorial supplement for the October issue of *The Transatlantic Review* and thus paid homage to his old colleague. According to Robert McAlmon, Ford compiled the Conrad supplement by sending telegrams to a number of writers inviting them to contribute an article on Conrad's place in English letters. McAlmon discovered that besides himself, Mary Butts and Hemingway had been thus invited and that all three of them thought their own article was to be the sole memorial essay. Ford had fairly good luck with his requests and along with Hemingway's printed McAlmon's, Mary Butts's, Ethel Colburn Mayne's, and his own, to which he added the first installment of his book about Conrad.

Hemingway took this opportunity to fulfill the task Ford had asked him to do in an editorial for the August issue, to comment on what the young people of the day thought of Conrad. In so writing, he paid his disrespects to newspaper editorialists, keeping in the fashion, T. S. Eliot, and literary technicians. The sum total of these attitudes, "Joseph Conrad,"

brought about if not the end of Hemingway's association with
Ford and his magazine, certainly the beginning of the end.

"What is there you can write about him now that he is
dead?" Hemingway asked rhetorically. He asserted that the
critics would dive — indeed were even then diving with the
agility and mass response of so many prairie dogs — into their
vocabularies and coming up with articles on Conrad's death.
Neither would a similar feat be hard for the editorial writers;
he proceeded to demonstrate, in a parody of an obituary
editorial, some of the fatuities that they would write. Among
the more advanced circle of his friends, he went on to point
out, it was fashionable to disparage Conrad; it might even
be dangerous for one's survival to admire him: "Living in a
world of literary politics where one wrong opinion often
proves fatal, one writes carefully." One could be made so
easily to feel he might be dropped from the party; for himself, for example, there was the short period of Coventry that
followed his remarking when speaking of George Antheil that
"I preferred my Stravinsky straight." Adding that he had
been more careful since, Hemingway immediately showed he
was now being the opposite by contrasting another favorite of
the party — Pound's party — with the deceased Conrad. Most
people he knew agreed that Conrad was a bad writer and
T. S. Eliot a good writer. On the contrary, wrote the sub-
editor of the *Review,* "if I knew that by grinding Mr. Eliot
into a fine dry powder and sprinkling that powder over Mr.
Conrad's grave Mr. Conrad would shortly appear, looking
very annoyed at the forced return, and commence writing I
would leave for London early tomorrow with a sausage
grinder. . . . you cannot couple T. S. Eliot and Joseph Conrad
in a sentence any more than you could see, say André Ger-
main and Manuel Garcia (Maera) walking down the street
together and not laugh."

Hemingway then recounted his reading of Conrad and
his responses to Conrad's fiction. He had read all of Conrad's books except *Lord Jim,* which he had not been able to
finish. Inasmuch as he could not reread Conrad, he guessed
that that quality might be what his friends meant when they
called Conrad a bad writer. But, asserted Hemingway, from
nothing else he had ever read had he gotten what every book
of Conrad had given him. Then came a reminiscence of the

way he had saved up four of Conrad's novels to read when he needed them badly, "when the disgust with writing, writers, and everything written of and to write would be too much." He had borrowed these volumes from a girl in Toronto, presumably during the preceding fall, when he had been in the process of deciding to leave journalism and to strike out on his own in Paris again. He had even bought three back numbers of the *Pictorial Review* and had avidly read the serialization of Conrad's last novel, *The Rover,* using up all his Conrad like a drunkard but excusing himself because he hoped that Joseph Conrad would write more stories: "He had lots of time." And now he was dead, "and I wish to God they would have taken some great, acknowledged technician of a literary figure and left him to write his bad stories." Within the surliness lay Hemingway's positive tribute to one of his masters, a tribute all the more effective for the irony and the air of brutality with which Hemingway conveyed it.

The attack on Eliot seemed then, and seems today, uncalled for, and — according to Burton Rascoe, in *We Were Interrupted* — Eliot angrily protested to Ford. In the "Chroniques" for the December number, the "Paris Letter: Editorial" carried Ford's rebuke. One gathers that whether Eliot had protested or not, there had been some rejoinders to Hemingway's verbal sausage grinding, for much of Ford's rambling editorial pleaded for generosity toward others, and he himself while admitting his partiality for the new school of writing, criticized the ferocity of Hemingway's attack. At the same time, the editor asserted, there must ordinarily be no tampering with what an author wrote: "These Chronicles we 'edit' only when attacks in them are made on countries to which their writers do not belong. As far as we are concerned any American may here attack America . . . The most ferocious of our correspondents having for instance this month made a quite gratuitous attack on one innocent and trusting nation, we have excised that paragraph. Next month another hand may be writing these notes." Hemingway had attacked the French in his August editorial and Eliot in the Conrad supplement. Probably Ford was telling those of his readers who could read between the lines that Hemingway's newsletters and editorial writing would no longer appear; and appear they did not for the rest of the publication of *The Transatlantic Review,* the lone number that came out, for January 1925.

The paragraph following his general explanation constituted Ford's direct apology to T. S. Eliot: "We wish we could reconcile it with our conscience to excise the paragraphs in which our chroniclers make attacks upon individuals. Thus two months or so ago" — the vagueness suggested no palliation of the offense — "one of these gentlemen made an attack on Mr. T. S. Eliot: he stated, that is to say, that he desired to grind Mr. T. S. Eliot into fine powder to be sprinkled on the shrine of another writer" (again, why the vagueness?). "We hesitated for a long time over the ethics of the matter, deciding in the end that our standards must prevail," that is, the standard of permitting one writer to attack another so long as both were Americans or French or British. "We had invited that writer to write, we had indicated no limits to his blood thirstyness: our hands fell powerless to our sides," he confessed in an elephantine travesty of a Jamesean figure. "We were besides convinced that Mr. Eliot does not mind. He does not" — an admission that Eliot *had* written something to the editor of the *Review.* "We take the opportunity of expressing for the tenth time our admiration for Mr. Eliot's poetry," a profession of faith that could not have poured water on this particular fire.

A final jab at Hemingway was the following announcement that "If the sub-editors permit it the end of the first part of *Some Do Not* will appear in this number," as the book had been published by Duckworth and was having some success. Hemingway was still scantily published, in contrast, and only Ford's generosity earlier in 1924 had provided the younger writer with an opportunity to advance his career through the *Review* Ford edited.

Bernard Poli sees "Joseph Conrad" as expressing hostility not only toward Eliot but toward Ford ("the great acknowledged technician of a literary figure") and Conrad. Another reader surely deplores the ethics behind the attack on Eliot, as well as its criticial common sense; but the identity of the great literary technician is veiled in anonymity — why select Ford? Why not Wells or Galsworthy? — and Hemingway's writing about Conrad in the essay indicates, by a strategy of irony, a definite admiration, in contrast to the reserva-

tions of such of his friends as Mary Butts and Robert Mc-
Almon. Hemingway here suggests that he admires Conrad
despite the fatuities of obituary praise, despite the distaste
of his friends and the dangers of breaking the rules of the pack
he ran with, and despite the condemnation of the critics.

The final months of the *Review* saw the appearance in it
of two stories by Hemingway. "The Doctor and the Doctor's
Wife" was published in the December 1924 issue, "Cross-
Country Snow" in the final issue in January 1925. Both stories reveal a precocity of talent even more astounding than
Fitzgerald's in 1920, and Hemingway now was beginning to
achieve a measure of recognition outside the Quarter's expatriate groups. Dr. Hemingway acknowledged his pleasure
when he read "The Doctor and the Doctor's Wife," despite
its being an uncomplimentary portrait of his wife, and in
return Hemingway said he was glad his father had liked the
Doctor story and explained he had used the real names of Dick
Boulton and Bill Tabeshaw in the story because he doubted
they would have access to a copy of *The Transatlantic Review*.
He added that he had written a number of stories about the
Michigan country and that the country was always true but
that what happened in the stories was fiction.

As Leicester Hemingway recounted this correspondence,
Hemingway in those months at the end of 1924 and the beginning of 1925 took his parents' opinions with some seriousness. He told them, for example, that the reason he had not
sent more samples of his work home was that Dr. and Mrs.
Hemingway prejudged his work with a puritanical viewpoint
and so had sent back their copies of *in our time*; it looked as
though they did not wish to see anything more.

Hemingway's explanations to his parents of his aims in
writing his Nick Adams stories show that he had not only
advanced as a technician (for all his contempt for that breed)
but also that he had formulated an aesthetic credo. He was
trying, he said, to get across, in all of his stories, the feeling
of actual life — not just to depict it or to criticize it. Readers
of the stories should actually experience the action and situation, but this could not be unless the stories encompassed the
bad and the ugly as well as the beautiful. If they took into
account only the beautiful, the reader could not believe it
because it would not be real. Only by showing both sides,

Hemingway told his father, only by putting in three dimensions and, if possible, four, could he achieve what he desired. His parents must also realize that as an artist their son was working toward a definite goal and that if some particular work seemed ugly or hateful, the next work might be one they liked very much. For all the simplicity of language, these statements embody a point of view toward the craft of writing that is rounded, workmanlike, highly defensible, and the product, obviously, of careful thinking.

"Cross-Country Snow," Hemingway's final story in the final number of the *Review* is one of the Nick Adams series. Beyond its own merits, discussed often enough, "Cross-Country Snow" is interesting because it is a picture of the adult Nick, skiing in the Alps and hindered by the pain of his war wound, a leg injury like Hemingway's own wound; and, like Hemingway, Nick is wistful because of his great missed chance, the experience of American college life. The story is about the skiing trips the Hemingways took in 1922 and 1923, before the advent of Bumby and the return to Toronto. George and Nick have, says Carlos Baker, something of a father-son relationship that recalls the similar pattern established between Dr. Henry Adams and Nick. The subject is not the joy of skiing but the joys of masculine friendship, from which women are excluded and which are threatened by marriage and children. At the end of "Cross-Country Snow," George and Nick realize they must say farewell to their days spent skiing together because Nick's wife Helen is pregnant and the Adamses must return to America, where, significantly, the skiing is not so good. But life disproved some part, at least, of the point of "Cross-Country Snow," for Hemingway did return to the Alps to ski, and in January 1925, just as the story appeared, he received word that Horace Liveright wished to publish an American edition of *In Our Time*, not merely the vignettes but the stories he had been writing too.

This turn of events was preceded by an autumn during which *The Transatlantic Review* gradually foundered. During July and August, when as a result of John Quinn's illness and death Ford was seeking another patron, Hemingway helped out by scouting prospective candidates. Gertrude Stein tells a story that one evening during the latter part of

1924, at the time when Hemingway was preparing his volume of short stories to submit to publishers in America, he turned up at her apartment with Evan Shipman, "an amusing boy who was to inherit a few thousand dollars when he came of age. He was not of age." Hemingway brought Shipman to the house of Gertrude Stein to talk about buying *The Transatlantic Review*. Shipman would buy the *Review* when he came of age, Hemingway is supposed to have informed Gertrude Stein and Alice Toklas. André Masson told them Shipman was to support a Surrealist review; and Juan Gris's wife Josette said Shipman would buy a house in the country when he came of age. As a matter of fact, concluded Gertrude Stein's anecdote, when Evan Shipman came of age nobody who had known him then seemed to know what he did with his inheritance.

In *A Moveable Feast* the story "Evan Shipman at the Lilas'" depicts Hemingway's friend in a far different light, not as a prospective patron of Ford's *Review* but as a desperately impecunious *jeune homme* too poor to afford a topcoat against the frosty nights of the Parisian autumn. Hemingway was better dressed for the fall than his friend, as he wore a sweatshirt for underwear and then a shirt and a blue wool French sailor's sweater over the shirt. Shipman was, remembered Hemingway, a fine poet, and he knew and cared about horses, writing, and painting. The portrait of Evan Shipman that Hemingway presents in his memoir possesses the careful detail of an Ingres sketch in pencil — or, perhaps rather, it has the fine yet bold detail of a sketch of the early 1920's by Adolf Dehn or Jean Louis Forain, sensitive, expressionist, slightly out of kilter, *A Young Poet down on His Luck*. Tall, pale, and skinny, Shipman was exquisitely dirty, wearing conventional middle-class clothes — a white shirt, a tie carefully knotted, a grey suit. But the suit was threadbare and wrinkled, the shirt was dirty and frayed, and the poet himself had dirty fingernails, tobacco-stained fingers, and a tight, deprecating smile that concealed bad teeth. The two friends so dissimilar superficially — Shipman thin, elegant, and dirty, Hemingway brawny, *fauve,* and fastidiously clean — frequented the Closérie des Lilas, where their favorite *garçon,* an old veteran named Jean, served them generous glasses of whisky. On Jean's free day, Shipman used to work

with him in the waiter's garden plot in Montrouge, out beyond the Porte d' Orléans.

Evan Shipman was a close friend of Harold Stearns, who
took him to his first trotting race in Paris, and an acquaintance of Nathan Asch. In the last days of the *Review*, when
Ford still owed Asch two hundred francs for a story, Asch
determined to collect his money. Meeting Shipman on the
way, Asch took him along to Ford's house. Shipman alleged
he had not eaten for a week and collapsed in mock-show. Ford
fed the weaker of his contributors beef broth and made out a
check for Asch, who recalled that Stella Bowen was aware
of Shipman's imposition and cast furious glances at both
young men.

It must have been due to Hemingway's good offices that
the *Review* published Evan Shipman's two poems — "Door-
ways" and an untitled long work — in the final number, along
with Donald Ogden Stewart's "Morning of Mrs. Gordon
Smythe," Tristan Tzara's "Seven Poems," and Hemingway's
"Cross-Country Snow." As a backer he had already faded
from the scene; he was to remain Hemingway's good friend,
however, long after their period of poverty had ended and
he had become a sports reporter.

Early in August, Hemingway had found Ford's only
replacement for John Quinn by introducing Mr. and Mrs.
Krebs Friend to the staff of the *Review*. The September issue
carried Krebs Friend's name as the new president of the
Transatlantic Review Company, and he contributed a "U.
S. Letter" to the "Chroniques" for October and a story,
scarcely more than an extended joke on the French, "The
French Wild Boar" to the December issue. Friend's "And
from the United States" was not the usual newsletter the
Review provided for its readers but a series of paragraphs
that are verbal practical jokes, as for example: "A Jesuit priest
came and told us about the world. It is like a hippodrome,
said he. Each cycle of life moves in a closed circle and accom-
plishes its end. Then another begins, but the canonical laws
will not allow me to pursue this question farther." In a similar vein, "The French Wild Boar" satirically relates the
author's hunt for a French wild boar, like the boars he had
formerly hunted in Kansas; but the hunt turns into a drinking party, and the narrator ends by shooting a crow on the

wing. Perhaps this black humor was to Hemingway's taste, but it could have been little to Ford's and Friend's contributions were wasted space in the *Review*.

Nathan Asch has said that in these months at the end of 1924 the *Review* was kept going by a very rich, very old lady who had just married Krebs Friend. He looked "like what later came to be known as *death warmed over*" and was a very young and confused war veteran, as Bernard Poli tells it, who had been rather badly shocked during the war. Mrs. Friend wished to give her husband an interest in life, though he wished more than anything to die. In an effort to hold him against the competition of other, younger women, Mrs. Friend dressed like a John Held, Jr., flapper, though as the difference between the pair was more than forty years, she also "wheezed and stumbled, actually being a very old lady, and she looked grotesque."

Nathan Asch's memory regarding the part the Friends played in Ford's famous parties would seem to be not altogether accurate when he says that it was for them, "with whom Ford was trying to ingratiate himself, that he gave his famous parties, the *bals* as the French say." The time table of that particular year does not accord with Asch's recollection. True, the action of *The Sun Also Rises* includes events of the summers of 1924 and 1925, but Hemingway seems to be consistent with the actual sequence of events of 1924 when he places the parties Mr. and Mrs. Braddocks gave at the *bal musette* as occurring before Jake Barnes and his gang went to the Pamplona fair. Moreover, as the Friends did not become important to *The Transatlantic Review* until late July or early August, they probably shared in the fun during the latter weeks of the parties Ford gave at the Bal Bullier, after the Hemingways and their friends had returned from Pamplona and had introduced the editor to his prospective patrons. By the middle of August, the great American rush to Le Havre and Cherbourg was on, because everybody who had a regular job must return to it by the Tuesday after Labor Day. So the dancings waxed most vertiginous that August, with the American tourists having a last fling before steaming back to the States, Prohibition, and bourgeois sobriety.

Life in Paris also took on a more sober cast. The Friends' rescue of the *Review* turned out to have the elements of

Krebs Friend's black humor. Since Mrs. Friend had all the money — she was reputed to be very rich — she had the final word in the affairs of *The Transatlantic Review*, and she ruined what there was left to ruin. Early in October Ernest Hemingway despondently wrote Gertrude Stein that he had had a constant fight to keep the *Review* being published, because Mrs. Friend had conceived the bright idea of cutting down on costs by attempting to drop all the contributions that must be paid for. As for Krebs Friend, his notion was to induce the young writers to contribute their work gratis and also to display their loyalty to the *Review* by soliciting advertising. Ford had had to sell shares in the Transatlantic Review Company to the Friends — the controlling interest — and now they controlled not only the pursestrings but the policy too. Hemingway had wanted Ford to take everything he could get from the new backers, but obviously Mr. and Mrs. Friend were more than an even match for the editor, as indeed were most people where money was concerned. Thus, despite Hemingway's warnings, Ford could not keep the Friends on the outside; very sensibly, they seemed to feel that if they must pay for the fun, they ought to share in it. Their way of sharing was to stop all expenditure, and Hemingway accurately forecast the end of *The Transatlantic Review* around the first of January 1925. At any rate, he told Gertrude Stein, it was some consolation to know that the *Review* would last out its full year.

In Marjorie Reid's view, in 1964, the Friends come out of the affair rather more likeably: they showed themselves ready to take over the financial management of the *Review*, as they did; but they relieved Ford of all "responsibilities." They stood ready to put the *Review* on a sound footing but not wholly as a philanthropy, as they expected it to be profitable and to attain status in the field of literary journals. But, recalled Ford's former secretary, the organization of the Transatlantic Review Company was about as nebulous as Krebs Friend's chance to earn prestige or dividends from the venture.

By September Ford was telling Gertrude Stein he had lost over a hundred thousand francs in supporting his magazine. Late in November, he refused to continue with the *Review* so long as the firm of Thomas Seltzer acted as the

American publisher. A Mrs. Putnam, apparently of New York, offered to help substantially, but Ford needed about $4500 to operate the magazine with for the first half of 1925, which meant raising three thousand dollars in the United States, and no such sum was forthcoming. So at the end of 1924 *The Transatlantic Review* sank in the quicksands of financial muddle.

Hemingway meanwhile was succeeding in publishing his work elsewhere. *The Little Review* remained loyal — fiercely and vocally loyal, as was its wont with those whom Margaret Anderson and Jane Heap admired. Its number dated Autumn-Winter 1924-25 published Hemingway's "Mr. and Mrs. Elliot," a return to Hemingway's satirical manner in his newsletters and editorials and even "A Divine Gesture," and a retrogression from the new manner of the vignettes of *in our time* and the three *Transatlantic* stories. Its main connection with these stories is the barely concealed element of the *roman à clef*. Like "Cross-Country Snow" and the newsletters, this story deals with the Parisian expatriates whom Hemingway traveled with. Hubert Elliot is a rich Bostonian who marries a Southern girl and settles with her into a chateau in Touraine. The trouble is that their ménage is a *ménage à trois*. Hubert Elliot wishes to write poetry and start a family, but Mrs. Elliot's girl friend, with whom she had operated a book store in the States before Hubert's advent, moves into the chateau, and Mrs. Elliot proves to be more interested in the friend than in her husband. The friend finds her niche in the Elliots' life by typing Mr. Elliot's poetry, and the master of the chateau attains success of a sort when he subsidizes a publisher to bring out a book of his poems. "In the evening they all sat at dinner together in the garden under a plane tree and the hot evening wind blew and Elliot drank white wine and Mrs. Elliot and the girl friend made conversation and they were all quite happy," which is to say they were the reverse.

Malicious as the story is, it expresses Hemingway's own misgivings about marriage, along with his other stories published at the time, "The Doctor and the Doctor's Wife," and "Cross-Country Snow." "Mr. and Mrs. Elliot" also displays Hemingway's usual antagonism toward T. S. Eliot, in the use of Eliot's name for the milksop character of Hubert Elliot;

and it embodies Hemingway's uneasiness about getting published. Would he be reduced to the ultimate indignity, shared by several of his acquaintances, of paying to see his stories published?

"Comment" in the same number of *The Little Review* gave Hemingway a helping puff. Under the subheading "Others," in a long paragraph of literary gossip, Margaret Anderson wrote up three friends, Djuna Barnes, Hemingway, and herself, in precisely the social-notes-from-all-over manner that Hemingway had satirized in Ford's *Review*: "Djuna Barnes is in Cagnes. She has recently finished a three-act play. Hemingway" — like Picasso or Joyce or Eliot, he is already being identified sufficiently by his surname — "is living in Paris, teaching his one-year-old son to bullfight. He is about to publish his first long book," a friendly prognostication of the American edition of *In Our Time*. And, finally, "Margaret Anderson is in Italy at the moment, she recently appeared in the Paris journal with an article on the 'Ulysses' trial and a criticism of the critics." "Comment" saved its Parthian shot for Ford Madox Ford. The irreverence of a four-page sheet on the death of Anatole France — entitled *A Rotten Corpse* and issued by "our young Frenchmen (all but one of them have appeared in the Little Review)" — was contrasted with Ford's "symposium on Conrad," in which "no one even went so far as to say he was an unfertilized egg. The one attitude is so French the other so US . . . the truth is that neither group cares a 'whoop' for any great man . . . but the Frenchmen have more fun" not caring. As "Comment" wisecracked, "Some think it better to let the French razz old dead Anatole — 'Some Do Not.' "

Along with that social-literary notice, the same number showed its awareness of Hemingway's trials; Jane Heap rallied to his side in his feud with Ford Madox Ford. Her "Reader Critic: A Letter from the Little Review to the Little Review" asked: "Did you see the announcement for the Pan-American number of *The Transatlantic Review*," that is to say, the September number that Hemingway edited, "and Ford's talk on what he is doing. . . . vellities [*sic*] of what we used to talk when we first started the L. R. and he is applauded as a 'modern' and listened to with interest. . . . because he is a man. Hemingway finds all the new stuff for him doesn't he? One gets madder every day! Give my love to the dear Brancusi." Miss Heap's boiling point was famously low, and the source of her anti-Ford sentiment is pretty obvious. She must have known, further, that active as he was on behalf of *The Transatlantic Review*, Hemingway was far from finding all the new stuff for its editor. She surely was aware, still further, that years before she had come to *The Little Review*, Ford Madox Ford had brilliantly edited his own *English Review*; but then he was a man, and that in itself provided Jane Heap the ground for other criticism.

Hemingway's differences with Ford thus became the stuff of general gossip. Burton Rascoe wrote in his memoir *We Were Interrupted* that after Ford's defense of T. S. Eliot in the *Review*, Hemingway severed his connection with the magazine and ceased to speak to Ford, although nightly they met in the same gathering places and Hadley Hemingway and the Fords remained on good terms. After dinner one evening Rascoe and his party went to a *bal musette* near the Panthéon where Ford introduced him to Nancy Cunard, E. E. Cummings, Robert McAlmon, and also, among others, to Mrs. Hemingway. Hemingway was there, but Ford and he were not speaking. Hemingway came up to Rascoe, whose favorable notice in "A Bookman's Day Book" he no doubt recalled favorably, and introduced himself. After Ford asked the Rascoes and Mrs. Hemingway to sit at a table with him, Hemingway is supposed to have said to his wife, "Pay for your own drinks, do you hear! Don't let him [nodding toward Ford] buy you anything."

It was difficult for Hemingway to parry Ford's thrusts, as Alice Toklas recalled in her memoir, *What Is Remembered*. One day at a party where Gertrude Stein was talking to Ford, Hemingway came up to speak to her. Ford wafted him away; "Go away, young man, it is I who am speaking to Miss Stein, do not interrupt me." And then Ford asked Gertrude Stein if he might dedicate his new book to her; she was delighted.

In his oblique way, so much in contrast to Hemingway's direct ferocity of attack, Ford called his farewell number of January 1925, "as irritatingly as possible," a "Children's Number," with Gertrude Stein, Havelock Ellis, and himself "parentally to gaze upon the firelit revels" of the holidays. He

pointed out that "in these columns Mr. McAlmon, Mr. Hemingway, and Mr. J. J. Adams made their first appearance before an international audience," a most pardonable inaccuracy
under the circumstances. And even the irritation of Ford's pa-
rental stance was quite right; as did so many of his friends,
then and afterward, he too was aware that Hemingway's antipathy sprang from the atavistic desire to rebel against one's
father, to bring down the old male in order to master the
entire herd.

Reviewing the course of the New Movement, spreading
"all over the Anglo-Saxon world from the West Middle West
of the United States to the West Middle West of the London
suburbs," Ford described the "very definite creative impulse"
as "pretty well kindred throughout" and "very much the
same tide in motion everywhere." His chief hope lay in the
promise of the young American writers, for the "young American suffers much less from bad models since he is a pioneer,"
while the "young Englishman much more" suffers "from the
ill-effects of class and of the worst possible models." A year
back *The Transatlantic Review* had set out with two main
objects in view, the promotion of greater cordiality in international relationships so that the arts might work in a better
atmosphere and the desire to provide a place for publishing
"such sincere commencing authors as the world might hold."
Ford asserted that he had not known even one of the contributors he had named — neither Adams, McAlmon, nor
Hemingway — when he began the *Review*, that without his
magazine "that creative work would in all human probability
have had to wait a great deal longer for its expression," and
that the *Review* was "the only organ in Anglo-Saxondom that
performs this particular function on a large scale and over a
large space of the earth's surface." He gave a brief explanation of the financial difficulties that were terminating publication and hopefully concluded that they would be sur-
mounted: "Then once more towards the spring, the *transatlantic review* will resume its tranquil voyagings."

His hope was not to be realized. Ford and Hemingway
would henceforth go their very different and separate ways,
the older man to another fifteen years of picaresque inse-
curity and the creation of his memoirs and his masterpiece,
the Tietjens series of novels, Hemingway to a quick and dazz-

ling success, the creation of a personal legend, and the long years of artistic drouth watered only by *The Old Man and the Sea* and *A Moveable Feast*. It was Ford Madox Ford who, in the larger sense, forgave. However he may have twitted the sensitivity of his quondam sub-editor in *It Was the Nightingale,* the older man invariably paid tribute to the younger. He wrote an appreciative preface to the Modern Library edition of *A Farewell to Arms* and near the end of his long career, in 1937, wrote in "There Were Strong Men," the last essay in his book *Portraits from Life,* that perhaps he had been wrong, that as Wyndham Lewis cried one day, it was foolish for the novelist to try to efface himself, to make people think there isn't any author and that they're living in the "affairs . . . you adumbrate, isn't that your word? What balls! What rot! . . . Efface yourself! . . . Bilge!" So in the end, Ford had to acknowledge the viability of the younger men's way of writing, as he had Wyndham Lewis express it. Of all these fellows, it was Hemingway who most successfully injected himself into his fiction, who refused to efface himself, who fused personal legend and work of art. Yet, in the same essay, Ford gave Hemingway his due and placed *A Farewell to Arms* as one of the novels by twelve authors — among them Jane Austen, Henry James, Mrs. Gaskell, Caroline Gordon, and Stephen Crane — whom he would read if he found himself on "a desert island Midway in the Atlantic."

Hemingway never forgot and never forgave; Ford was, even beyond the grave (both his own and Hemingway's) an ignoble presence with an unendurably bad smell.

What an irony! It surely seemed back in January 1925 that the dreary little feud would be nothing to become excited about, nothing more significant than dozens of similar causes for comment in the gossip columns of *The Little Review*. Ford was an established, distinguished man of letters, dubious perhaps where women and money were concerned and given to fancifying, but nevertheless a man of personal courage and proven talent. Ernest Hemingway was just another Bohemian of the Quarter, living off his wife's small capital, trying to make a name for himself by writing stories that few editors would accept and poems that were in the most questionable taste.

He was, also, though few seemed to recognize the quality

at the time, one of those extremely rare men who have both
the talent and the strength of character to force the world to
recognize, then to acclaim their peculiar excellence — in Hemingway's case, his excellence as a stylist, as a story-teller,
and as the voice of his generation, *une génération perdue*.
That force, which made Ernest Hemingway a legend before
he was thirty, received its due recognition for the first time
when, making good his promise of a year earlier, Edmund
Wilson reviewed *3 Stories & 10 Poems* and *in our time* in *The
Dial* for October 1924.

CHAPTER 6

"MR HEMINGWAY'S poems are not particularly important, but his prose is of the first distinction. He must be counted as the only American writer but one — Mr Sherwood Anderson — who has felt the genius of Gertrude Stein's Three Lives and has been evidently influenced by it. Indeed, Miss Stein, Mr Anderson, and Mr Hemingway may now be said to form a school by themselves." These salvoes opening Edmund Wilson's review, "Mr Hemingway's Dry-Points," of *3 Stories & 10 Poems* and *in our time* mark the real beginning of Hemingway's American reputation. Despise the critics though he might, Ernest Hemingway must always feel indebted to Wilson's generous prescience, given the authority and glamor of publication in *The Dial*. The praise was all the sweeter for Scofield Thayer's having rejected Hemingway's poetic "things" two and a half years previously.

According to Edmund Wilson, the chief characteristic of the Stein-Anderson-Hemingway school was "a naïveté of language often passing into the colloquialism of the character dealt with which serves actually to convey profound emotions and complex states of mind." This was, said Wilson, a distinctively American development in prose — as opposed to more or less successful American achievements in the traditional style of English prose — which artistically justified itself at its best as a limpid shaft into deep waters. He thus saw Hemingway not as imitative but as strikingly original and as almost having invented in the "dry little vignettes" of *in our time* "a form of his own" that was "remarkably successful in suggesting moral values by a series of simple statements." Wilson's feeling was that below its cool objective manner *in our time* really constituted a harrowing record of barbarities. Hemingway was "wholly unperturbed as he tells about these things: he is not a propagandist even for humanity. His bull-fight sketches have the dry sharpness and elegance of the bull-fight lithographs of Goya. And, like Goya, he is concerned first of all with making a fine picture. He is showing you what life is, too proud an artist to simplify."

It was a mistake on the part of someone on the staff of *The Dial* (Alyse Gregory? She, at any rate, had succeeded Gilbert Seldes as managing editor with the issue for February 1924) to entitle Wilson's review "Mr Hemingway's Dry-Points." Goya's medium for his *Tauromachia* of 1815-16 was etching with aquatint, in which he reigned supreme in his age but also in which he was, obviously, the follower of Rembrandt, while in the great *Bulls of Bordeaux* of 1825, Goya displayed his innovative power as one of the earliest masters of the then novel medium of lithography. (Even here the title of the review was inexact: the line of an etching is made with the point of a needle tipped in acid and scratched through a special wax onto a metal plate, after which the waxed plate is immersed in an acid solution, and the wax is dissolved in a solvent; as with an engraving, the line of a dry-point is scratched into the plate, but a dry needle instead of a burin is used, and the metal plate is not burnished smooth to receive the impression of the paper.) Wilson had said in his review that Hemingway, like Goya, was "original." To suggest that Hemingway, however talented, was working in a well-established tradition was to miss the point of the review; by comparing his stories to Goya's etchings, the title, "Mr Hemingway's Dry-Points," did less than justice to either Hemingway or Wilson.

Wilson's general judgment was that Hemingway's "little

book has more artistic dignity than any other that has been written by an American about the period of the war"; it was "not perhaps the most vivid book, but the soundest." After that praise of an unknown writer, which, conceivably, may have seemed extravagant to most readers of *The Dial*, it mattered little that the reviewer expressed qualifications about the poems and about "the paleness, the thinness," of some of the effects, as with the story "Up in Michigan," or that he disliked the otherwise very pretty and amusing cover of *in our time* because the titles were throughout printed without capitals. Here, however, Wilson was criticizing William Bird's typographical design rather than Hemingway's writing. This device of printing in lower case only, "which used to be rather effective when the modernists first used to use it to call attention to the fact that they had something new to offer," by the fall of 1924 had grown "common and a bore." Moreover, the American advertisers had taken it over as one of their stock tricks: "And it is so unsightly in itself that it is rather a pity to see it become — as in the case of Mr Hemingway's book and Mr Hueffer's 'transatlantic review' — a sort of badge of everything that is freshest and most interesting in modern writing."

Even in his qualifications, Wilson was generous in estimating Hemingway's talent — linking him with Ford was meant to be a compliment — and the review was unique in its day as the sole critique of the writer's beginning work by a responsible American of the vanguard and in a leading American literary journal. One indication of the importance of the review, for both Hemingway and *The Dial*, is that the editors placed it in the regular section of signed book reviews and did not relegate either title reviewed to the section of "Briefer Mention," where the unsigned short reviews of one paragraph appeared and where short notices were bound to languish in comparative obscurity.

What next occurred in Hemingway's relations with *The Dial* is, if ambiguous, not unparalleled in the annals of literature. Before Edmund Wilson's laudatory review appeared in *The Dial* for October 1924, Ernest Hemingway sent a group of what, in the 1930's he called his "obscene" poems — among them one attacking *The Dial* — to *Der Querschnitt*. This brilliant German counterpart of *The Dial* had been

founded in Berlin in 1920 by Alfred Flechtheim, head of the
famous Berlin publishing house Propyläen-Verlag, and was
edited in the middle 1920's by Hans von Wedderkop, an
editor as distinguished as the founder. An even more sophisticated if also more raffish monthly than *The Dial, Der Querschnitt* was similar to the American journal in its cosmopolitan taste, its espousal of the vanguard, and its practice of
publishing pictures of contemporary art; some of these reproduced works from the publisher's Galerie Flechtheim in
Berlin, which also furnished such pictures to *The Dial* occasionally and from which Scofield Thayer made a number of
important purchases for his Dial Collection. Besides the
staple reading fare in German, von Wedderkop gave his sub-
scribers an occasional piece in French or English. His editorial policy was as cosmopolitan as Ford Madox Ford's and
represented the best values of the Weimar republic.

Wedderkop's Paris literary scout in 1924 was a young
American, the pianist and composer George Antheil. Even
younger than Hemingway, Antheil had arrived in Paris after
a year or two in Germany. His memoir of 1947, *Bad Boy of
Music,* describes his life in the Quarter and his making friends
with the artists and musicians and writers who lived there,
mostly the Americans led by Pound who met daily in Sylvia
Beach's bookshop, Shakespeare and Company, near the Odéon.
As members in good standing of the international vanguard,
Sylvia Beach's friends and customers were acquainted with
Der Querschnitt and Hans von Wedderkop; they dubbed him
"Mr. Awfully Nice" because his spoken English apparently
was confined to the two words "awfully nice."

In *Bad Boy of Music,* Wedderkop is represented as having
approached Antheil because he had heard, erroneously, that
the composer had been an assistant editor of some kind on
The Little Review, a journal the German editor admired
inordinately. In any case, he got in touch with Antheil, who,
needing the money, agreed to act for *Der Querschnitt.* When
his editor asked for material, Antheil went to Sylvia Beach,
Ford Madox Ford, and Ezra Pound and asked them to help
him out. The first manuscript he sent to Wedderkop was a
group of five poems from James Joyce's *Chamber Music* which
Der Querschnitt promptly printed in October 1923.

One of Antheil's music pupils during this time was an

American boy named George O'Neil, son of a prominent lumberman from the Pacific Coast and brother of the actress Barbara O'Neil. Young O'Neil had another tutor for English composition, boxing, and skiing — Ernest Hemingway. Somehow Hemingway and Antheil got to be friends, and one day Hemingway took his colleague home to show him a whole typescript sheaf of stories never before published. The Paris scout for *Der Querschnitt* immediately thought of Wedderkop, and while Hemingway was not very anxious to give over his stories for publication in a German magazine, Antheil at last got Sylvia Beach and Ezra Pound to prevail upon him: "Wedderkop published it serially without further ado." Antheil's account is not to be taken literally, and this writing is not related to either the Paris or the New York edition of *In Our Time*; but it may well be true that he was the agent through whom Wedderkop secured the four poems and the story, "The Undefeated," that Hemingway published in 1924-25 in *Der Querschnitt*.

In his book of personal experiences on safari in East Africa, *The Green Hills of Africa*, Hemingway recalled in 1935 the magazine that had published his verses during the fall and winter of 1924-25. Traveling through the African bush one night, Hemingway meets a short, bandy-legged man named Kandisky, dressed in Tyroler hat, leather shorts, and open shirt. They introduce themselves by name, and Kandisky says that Hemingway is a name he has heard: "Where? Where have I heard it? Oh, yes. The *dichter*. You know Hemingway the poet?" When asked where he has read Hemingway *der Dichter*, Kandisky replies, "In the *Querschnitt*." Hemingway the hunter accepts the identification and explains in an aside to the reader that *Der Querschnitt* "was a German magazine I had written some rather obscene poems for, and published a long story ["The Undefeated"] in, years before I could sell anything in America." (This last statement is not correct, for Wedderkop accepted "The Undefeated" at about the time Boni and Liveright agreed to bring out the augmented American edition of *In Our Time*.) Kandisky, there in the middle of the African bush, engages Hemingway in a conversation about the writers for *Der Querschnitt* — Joachim Ringelnatz, who wrote rather scurrilous satiric verses; Heinrich Mann; Rainer Maria Rilke; Paul Val-

éry; and James Joyce — and he thanks Hemingway: "there
are things we do not agree on. But it is a pleasure to meet one
of the great old *Querschnitt* group."

A quarter of a century later, Hemingway used the story
"Hunger Was Good Discipline" in *A Moveable Feast* to touch
on his relations with *Der Querschnitt*, its editor, and George
Antheil. He depicts himself as wandering, broke and rather
hungry, one afternoon into Sylvia Beach's bookshop, Shakespeare and Company — which he used as a mail drop in those
days — and asking whether any mail had arrived for him.

At first Sylvia Beach is dubious, but she opens a door in
her desk and hands Hemingway a letter that feels as though
it has money in it. "Wedderkop," she says.

"It must be from *Der Querschnitt*," Hemingway agrees.
"Did you see Wedderkop?"

"No. But he was here with George. He'll see you. Don't
worry. Perhaps he wanted to pay you first."

"It's six hundred francs. He says there will be more."

To which Sylvia Beach responds with "Dear Mr. Awfully
Nice."

Hemingway is puzzled that Germany should be the only
place he can sell his work, to *Der Querschnitt* and to the leading liberal newspaper, the *Frankfurter Zeitung*. Sylvia teases
him by remarking that he can always sell stories to Ford; but
Hemingway points out that at the rate of thirty francs a page
paid by *The Transatlantic Review*, Ford would have to publish one of his stories five pages long every three months, making a hundred and fifty francs a quarter, in order to total the
sum that Hans von Wedderkop had just paid. Hemingway's
complaint to Sylvia Beach is that while he can write his stories, nobody will buy them: "There is no money coming in
since I quit journalism." Her reply is that he should not
worry, because as an inkling of what the future holds, he
already has been paid for a story that *Der Querschnitt* has
bought.

The incident is intended to reveal Hemingway's financial struggle in 1924, but what it fails to explain is that
while Hemingway must have been paid by Wedderkop for
four poems, published over three issues of *Der Querschnitt*,
only one story, "The Undefeated," was published, and that
in German translation. Hemingway told Harold Loeb that

Wedderkop said the story was marvelous; but his letter to Loeb was dated January 5, 1925, and it gives no indication of what Wedderkop paid Hemingway for the four poems he took for *Der Querschnitt,* which the magazine had already published. The financial blank is not filled in by John Dos Passos' casual remark that *in our time* had earned its author acclaim in *recherché* circles but no cash and that Hemingway's "main source of income was writing smutty poems for a German magazine called *Der Querschnitt.*" ("We got all the fun there was out of that name," Dos Passos added.)

Hemingway's poem attacking *The Dial* was his first contribution to appear in Wedderkop's magazine. Entitled "The Soul of Spain with McAlmon and Bird the Publishers," it was serialized in *Der Querschnitt,* with Part I appearing in the issue for October 1924 and Parts II-VI in the next issue, for November. In Part I, the narrator uses the repetitive technique of Gertrude Stein to speak his piece against Democracy, relativity, dictators, H. L. Mencken, Waldo Frank, Harold Loeb's little magazine *Broom,* Dada, Jack Dempsey. Each is "the shit"; however, this list, Hemingway assures the readers of *Der Querschnitt,* is not a complete one:

They say Ezra is the shit.
But Ezra is nice.
Come let us build a monument to Ezra.
Good a very nice monument.
You did that nicely.
Can you do another?
Let me try and do one.
Let us all try and do one.
Let the little girl over there in the corner try and do one.
Come on little girl.
Do one for Ezra.
Good.
You have all been successful children.
Now let us clean the mess up.
The Dial does a monument to Proust.
We have done a monument to Ezra.
A monument is a monument.
After all it is the spirit of the thing that counts.

The excremental monument to Ezra Pound is equated with the monument *The Dial* did to Marcel Proust, and the allusion was to very recent literary history. Though Scofield Thayer may never have called Ezra a shit, he did on one occasion term Pound's translation of Rémy de Gourmont's *Dust for Sparrows* — while much to the editor's discontent it was running wellnigh interminably in *The Dial*, from September 1920 through May 1921 — "Shit for Sparrows"; and in that judgment Thayer was upheld by D. H. Lawrence, who complained to the editor that the sparrow dust was rubbish. Thayer's unwary remark in a routine letter to the *Dial* staff may well have reached Pound, and Pound's circle.

Especially gratuitous, on the surface, was Hemingway's lumberingly satirical attack on the more public matter of the relationship of Proust and *The Dial*. From its first year under Scofield Thayer and Sibley Watson, *The Dial* had advocated Proust's novel. In October 1920 appeared an anonymous English translation of "Saint-Loup: A Portrait," from *À la Recherche du temps perdu*, accompanied by Richard Aldington's critique, "The Approach to M. Marcel Proust." The novelist's death occasioned two memorial essays in *The Dial*: in March 1923, Malcolm Cowley's "A Monument to Proust," and in May 1923, Francis Birrell's more ambivalent "Marcel Proust: The Prophet of Despair." "The Dial does a monument to Proust": how closely Hemingway must have followed *The Dial*, how keenly he must have resented Scofield Thayer's dismissal of those early poems, when, so many months later, he went out of his way to incorporate in "The Soul of Spain" the title of Malcolm Cowley's tribute to Proust. It is quite possible, in fact, that the poem was intended to attack Cowley, who had met Hemingway through Pound in the summer of 1923, as well as Proust; Cowley pretty regularly published in *The Dial*, and such success was cause enough for Hemingway's scorn. "After all it is the spirit of the thing that counts": by equating, in spirit, Cowley's monument to Proust with the monument to Ezra done by the children in Hemingway's verses, the poet both privately settled an old score to his satisfaction and more openly defended Pound against the Editor of *The Dial*. Whatever one thought about the policy of *The Dial*, Proust was one writer to whom this prestigious magazine had erected a monument, to whom it had paid homage. In contrast, Ezra Pound — not only a recognized leader of the literary vanguard but Hemingway's good friend — got as his reward from *The Dial* the loss of his job as Paris Correspondent and literary agent for the magazine.

The same October issue of *Der Querschnitt* carried another poem by Hemingway, "The Earnest Liberal's Lament," as gamy as "The Soul of Spain" but mercifully much briefer. In this lament the speaker admits his knowledge that monks masturbate at night, pet cats screw, and some girls bite — sexual felonies all, in his view. And yet, he concludes, what can I do to set things right? Hemingway does catch the querulous tone of the aggrieved rationalist, the earnest liberal, who cannot understand why the world persists in its irrational wickedness. By transferring the subject from men's political to their sexual frailties, Hemingway makes his point. By talking bawdy, he inspires a ripple of shock; perhaps our political peccadillos are as irremediable and adamant to correction as our sexual itch. The raucous phallic comedy of the lines soon made them well known across the ocean in Greenwich Village. Early in 1925, at a meeting and dinner party of the "Esthetes" — largely composed of the staff of *Broom* and its friends — to plan a successor to *Broom* tentatively entitled *Esthetes 1925*, Harold Loeb listened to Allen Tate's recitation of Hemingway's ditty; the whole crowd joined in the last line as chorus. Somebody asked Loeb whether he knew Hemingway. Sure, he knew Hemingway.

The next issue of Wedderkop's magazine published the second and final installment of "The Soul of Spain with McAlmon and Bird the Publishers," Parts II-VI. Here Hemingway gets down to the business of writing about Spain. The soul of Spain is the "cruel sport," the bullfight. To convey the very essence of Spain, Hemingway avails himself of the technique of the Dadaist prose poem, in which the elements of expressionism and of linguistic burlesque are basic to its conception. In that respect "Part Two of the Soul of Spain" remains unique among Hemingway's published writing, for in this work he more obviously exploits the technical innovations of Dada than he ever had done previously or would do later. To be sure, much of the poem also parodies the writing of Gertude Stein, perhaps even more obviously than it parodies Dada; but both the "black" wit of the verbal play and the expressionist element of symbol-making, akin to Imagism, reveal the pastiche of Dada.

The burlesque of Gertrude Stein's writing is exemplified in the sixth part of the poem. "A Serious and Vivid
Account of a Dramatic Moment in the Cruel Sport." Here
Hemingway brilliantly condenses all his observation of the
tragedy of the bullring into three brief paragraphs. The first
is a vignette of the fatal wounding and the killing of the bull,
a subject no different from certain images from *in our time*,
but related in the superficially chaotic unpunctuated constructions of Dada and Gertrude Stein. It ends with "They
are going to kill him back of the horns with the short knife."
The second paragraph is one sentence long, and in the reitera-
tive cadences of Gertrude Stein, it takes up where the previous
sentence leaves off: "Short knives are thick short knives are
quick short knives make a needed nick." Hemingway trans-
formed the Steinian nonsense, of course, and used its aural
patterning to convey his image by means of a logical verbal
construction not essentially different from many of Gerard
Manley Hopkins's. The final paragraph, of two sentences,
constitutes at once a pause and a comment on the preceding
bloody, tragic act: "Women love to see the puntillo used. It
is exactly like turning off an electric light bulb." Here Dada
with its puzzling allusiveness (which somehow made supra-
verbal sense), *Othello* ("Put out the light, and then put out
the light"), the cruel sport, a most involved sexual frisson,
and violent death rush together and fuse in one black-and-
white image. The light goes out, the poem ends. In this foreshadowing of Picasso's *Guernica*, Hemingway made sufficient
amends for the sleaziness of much of the other material he
gave to Wedderkop to publish.

The November 1924 issue of *Der Querschnitt* printed
another of Hemingway's poems about literary life, "The
Lady Poets with Foot Notes." The accompanying illustration, in the upper half of the page, was Matisse's pen-
and-ink sketch of a charmingly languorous odalisque. The
brief poem beneath was a pasquinade on the private
lives and professional talents and achievements of six
unidentified women writers; one guesses at Edna St. Vincent Millay, Aline Kilmer, Sara Teasdale, Zoe Akins, Lola
Ridge, and Amy Lowell. In the time-hallowed manner of
"This Little Pig Went to Market," Hemingway described
each woman in a sentence constituting a line of verse, to which

was appended a footnote further limning the subject of the line. The last sentence described a person who undoubtedly was Amy Lowell: "One lady poet was big and fat and no fool." The appended footnote added: "She smoked cigars all right, but her stuff was no good."

This is a literary burlesque, its objects not only the lady poets themselves but also the manner of their portrayal. As with Hemingway's earlier verse satire, the technique, borrowed from such disparate sources as the writings of Gertrude Stein, Mother Goose, and T. S. Eliot (the Eliot of *The Waste Land*), also owed something to Marianne Moore's poetry. Indeed, whatever Hemingway's intention may have been, the poem as published would inescapably remind readers after 1924 of Miss Moore's poems because of the visual device of the appended footnotes. Until the end of 1924, Marianne Moore was not a well-known lady poet with footnotes. Not until her *Observations*, published on December 27, 1924, did she append in a book of her poetry a section of notes indicating sources of some allusions and quotations in the poems of the volume. Yet despite the apparent difficulty offered by the dates for the publication of "The Lady Poets with Footnotes" and *Observations*, these need cause no insurmountable objection to the argument that Hemingway was poking fun at Marianne Moore's custom of appending footnotes to poems. He probably knew from his friend Robert McAlmon that Marianne Moore learnedly incorporated portions of other work more or less directly into her poems; at the McAlmons', Hemingway may have seen some of her work in manuscript, since McAlmon's wife, the novelist Winifred Bryher, was a good friend of Miss Moore's and had, with H. D., edited and seen into print Miss Moore's first collection, the *Poems* of 1921. Further, Hemingway may have heard about the appended section of "Notes" to *Observations* through the McAlmons or similarly may have even seen proofs of the volume in advance of publication. In any case, he was acquainted with Miss Moore's work about the time "The Lady Poets with Footnotes" came out.

At the end of 1924, Miss Moore held a unique place as a contributor to *The Dial*. Her *Observations* was being published by Thayer's newly formed Dial Press coincidentally with his announcement of her reception of the Dial Award.

In *The Dial* for January 1925 came the editorial announcement that she was the recipient of the Dial Award for 1924,
with a eulogy written by Thayer himself and serialized for
January-February-March 1925. And on April 27, 1925, Miss
Moore began her association with *The Dial* as one of its staff,
first as managing editor, then as editor until its cessation in
July 1929.

Given Edmund Wilson's pioneering review of the early
stories, one understands why, for a second time, Hemingway tried his luck with *The Dial* now. Perhaps hoping too
that his remarks about the magazine and several of its contributors in *Der Querschnitt* would not have been reported
back to Scofield Thayer (who had been in New York since
August 1923), Hemingway submitted a second manuscript
to *The Dial* in October or November 1924. Apparently un-
aware of his earlier rejection, Alyse Gregory, as managing
editor, sent the story back to the author with a brief letter of
rejection dated December 4, 1924. The title of Hemingway's
story is not in the letter; Miss Gregory merely said that she was
returning the story that the staff had enjoyed but that they
did not find wholly suited to their present needs; and she
civilly added her thanks to the author for having given *The
Dial* the opportunity of considering his story. Alyse Gregory
could not recall ever having seen this particular story by Hemingway and in a letter of January 5, 1965, declared that she
recalled one occasion but not two on which she was editorially
responsible for writing submitted by Hemingway. The sole
evidence is the carbon copy of her letter of December 4,
1924, now among the Dial Papers housed in the Beinicke
Library at Yale.

Undaunted by a second rejection from *The Dial*, Hemingway tried it a third time. on January 21, 1925. His neatly
written letter, with its careful stipulation that four francs in
postal coupons were enclosed for return postage, was designed
to please the most captious of lady editors. On the other hand,
the writer's explanation for the state of his typescript — that
it had been sent to a friend in Spain to read and had been
rather mangled in the post — would probably meet with a
negative shrug from a busy editor accustomed to glance at
thousands of manuscripts from hopeful authors. Hemingway
went on to explain further that as it would cost nearly 300

francs to have the story retyped and as he had not earned that much during the past year by his writing, he trusted Miss Gregory to overlook the disreputable condition of the type-script submitted. The pathos of that admission was perhaps somewhat vitiated by the address from which the story was mailed, the Hotel Taube, Schruns, in the Austrian skiing district of the Vorarlberg.

The Taube, though cheap with its pension rate of two dollars a day for the three Hemingways seeking escape from the winter dreariness of Paris, had large, comfortable rooms with big windows and with the Alpine amenities of huge stoves and great beds piled with warming blankets and feather coverlets. "The meals were simple and excellent and the dining room and the woodplanked public bar were well heated and friendly." Thus Hemingway remembered the early months of 1925 in "There Is Never Any End to Paris," the final story of those comprising *A Moveable Feast*. As with the other stories in the book, "There Is Never Any End to Paris" carefully melds times, and Hemingway in it combined the winter of 1923-24, in which he and his first wife and their baby, "Mr. Bumby" (John Hemingway), crossed the Atlantic in January 1924, with the early portion of 1925, when he was skiing at Schruns and writing stories. Hemingway thought of Schruns as a good place to work. He remarked in *A Moveable Feast* that he did his most difficult job of rewriting there when he revised the first draft of *The Sun Also Rises* and made it into a novel, at the beginning of 1926. He added that he could not remember which stories he wrote there but that several stories he wrote at Schruns turned out well.

Here, in his posthumously published recreation of his early days as a writer, Ernest Hemingway uses again, as he had used for many years — for example, with *A Farewell to Arms* and "The Snows of Kilimanjaro" — the opposition of mountain and plain. Paris was the city of the plain in the Proustian sense, despite its attractions and perhaps even because of those attractions: the drunkards in the sleazy Mouffe-tard district, the women in the bistros, the bohemian feck-lessness, the races at Longchamps. Schruns was the good life of work and skiing and fidelity to the beloved, spoiled only when intruders from Paris entered on the scene and by their

corruptness succeeded in seducing the young hero and breaking up his marriage. Much of this is alluded to in "The Snows
of Kilimanjaro," in the Joycean stream-of-consciousness reve-
ries and ravings of the dying protagonist Harry. "You loved
it there," Harry's wife assured him, of Paris. And he replied
that love was a dunghill, himself the cock that got on it to
crow. Dying, Harry told himself that he had never written
about the Paris he had cared about; much less mordantly, in
the romantic mist of recollection, Hemingway did write about
that Paris in *A Moveable Feast*. But the contrast he used in
his fiction, between the essential purity, the spiritual quality
of the mountains and the essential human corruption of the
city of the plain was only tangentially exploited in the first
story in which he used the mountains, the Alps, as a major
locale: "Cross-Country Snow." Not until *A Farewell to
Arms* does the theme emerge as a leading leitmotif in Hemingway's art.

Hemingway concluded his letter to Alyse Gregory by con-
gratulating *The Dial* on making its award to Marianne Moore.
Again one notes that he was still reading the magazine carefully and promptly: Thayer's announcement of the Dial
Award was placed at the rear of the January 1925 issue, the
first of the three installments of the Editor's eulogy of Miss
Moore, and since *The Dial* was regularly issued about two
weeks in advance of the month of publication, Hemingway
must have written to Miss Gregory shortly after receiving and
reading through his copy of the magazine for January 1925.
Why he mentioned Miss Moore in favorable terms so soon
after publishing "The Lady Poets with Foot Notes" is anybody's guess. Certainly a desire to propitiate or to curry favor
is not out of the question.

However he tried to please, the story was rejected. Alyse
Gregory disliked it. Both Scofield Thayer and Sibley Watson voted to accept it nevertheless, and so it was sent to an
outside reader for the deciding opinion. By one of those
ironies that novelists hesitate to employ for fear of being dis-
believed, their oracle was none other than — Marianne Moore!
"Since you and Mr Thayer have discussed Hemingway, Mr
Thayer thought you might be willing to give your judgment
of this manuscript which Mr Thayer and Dr Watson and
Miss Gregory disagree upon," wrote a member of the *Dial*

staff to Miss Moore. Next day, Marianne Moore replied: "I
have read Mr. Hemingway's story with great interest," but as
it stands, "I would say no." Could Miss Moore have been a
constant reader of *Der Querschnitt?*

In her letter of rejection on March 10, 1925, Alyse
Gregory began by apologizing for tardiness in returning his
story to Hemingway and went on to say how much the staff
regretted not being able to use it. Her reason for rejecting
the story was that *The Dial* was more than ever overburdened
with accepted material and that the staff did not see how they
could fit in Hemingway's piece. A final unwitting slice of
the editorial scalpel was Miss Gregory's expression of pleasure over Hemingway's approval of Miss Moore as the recipient of the Dial Award. Years later, in a letter of January
5, 1965, Miss Gregory said she feared her dislike of Hemingway's story was predominantly emotional: she *abhorred* bullfighting and never could abide this aspect of Hemingway, but
wasn't the real sin that of not having the prescience to bet
on the winning horse? And to another correspondent she
wrote: "You can blame me for the rejection of the Hemingway story. . . . It was a story about bull fighting. I *loathe* his
Death in the Afternoon. . . . However, it is always a mistake,
if not a calamity, not to back the winning horse."

One speculation about the story Hemingway submitted
to *The Dial* in January 1925 is that it was "The Undefeated,"
Hemingway's portrait of the wounded but indomitable torea-
dor Manuel Garcia. Perhaps after George Antheil sent a
copy of "The Undefeated" to Hans von Wedderkop and, of
course, before its appearance in *Der Querschnitt,* Ernest Hemingway decided to try his luck for the third and last time
with *The Dial.* To accept a story under such circumstances
was not unusual for the magazine; Hemingway was following
the practice of von Hofmannsthal, Mann, and Proust, all of
whom *The Dial* had republished in translation, at once paying
them for republication at reduced rates and introducing their
work to a cultivated American readership. And had the
response of *The Dial* to "The Undefeated" been favorable, it
would have been the first American magazine to publish a
Hemingway masterpiece; Edward J. O'Brien, more responsive
to Hemingway's talent, selected it for his *Best Short Stories
of 1926.*

Der Querschnitt, at any rate, continued to be receptive to Hemingway's work. In February 1925 it published the fourth and final poem of Hemingway's that Wedderkop took, "The Age Demanded," perhaps the best known of all his verses because it expresses the attitude of Jake Barnes's set in *The Sun Also Rises*. Nothing could be more period, more Lost-Generation, than the combination of toughness, irony, and self-pity of the eight lines that conclude:

> The Age demanded that we dance
> And jammed us into iron pants.
>
> And in the end the age was handed
> The sort of shit that it demanded.

The inspiration for the title and the poem's refrain was, fittingly, the second of the lyric poems in Ezra Pound's great sequence about the first World War, *Hugh Selwyn Mauberly*. Pound had cursed the times that brought on the war in which young men had walked "eye-deep in hell" and that treasured the tawdry cheapness of commercialism. "The age demanded an image," sang Pound, "Of its accelerated grimace"; and, echoing his master, "The age demanded that we sing," wrote Hemingway, "And cut away our tongue."

Meanwhile, across the Atlantic, the New York publishing house of Boni and Liveright decided to accept *In Our Time* — not the edition brought out by William Bird but one rearranged and augmented by ten stories. Harold Loeb asked Beatrice Kaufman, who was reading manuscripts for the firm, what had been decided, and when she gave him an affirmative answer, he cabled Hemingway the good news. Hemingway replied on February 27, the day he received Loeb's cable. Then ensued a comedy of errors. While such well-wishers as Sherwood Anderson (who after much backing and filling was gradually moving toward a contract with Boni and Liveright) and Harold Loeb had worked to persuade Horace Liveright to accept *In Our Time*, Scott Fitzgerald, although he had not yet met Hemingway, had already been urging his own editor, Maxwell Perkins of Scribner, to get in touch with Hemingway immediately. It was Edmund Wilson, Fitzgerald's classmate at Princeton, who had introduced Fitzgerald to Hemingway's work; so, as he had halfway promised he would, Wilson was trying to persuade the publishers to take a chance on some prose of the first distinction. But before Scribner could get in touch with Hemingway, still in the Vorarlberg skiing, Boni and Liveright signed him up, accepting *In Our Time* on the condition that he give them an option on his first three books. If they refused the second book, they forfeited rights to the third; the provisions of this contract, adds Carlos Baker, were to have important consequences in the history of Hemingway's publication in the United States. More importantly in March 1925, because of the advance of two hundred dollars he had received from Boni and Liveright for *In Our Time,* Hemingway was modestly solvent.

Not until its issues for June and July 1925 did *Der Querschnitt* publish "The Undefeated." Perhaps the lapse of time between late 1924, when Wedderkop accepted the story, and the summer of 1925, when he serialized it in two parts, was due to the problem of translating it. The translator was B. Bessmertny, the German title was "Stierkampf," and the first portion, in *Der Querschnitt* for June, was illustrated. Hemingway's rolls of film, which his "Pamplona Letter" in *The Transatlantic Review* mentioned, were thus very useful, disproving the skepticism Hemingway's cousin had displayed in the "Pamplona Letter" about the quality of his photographs of the *corrida.* Wedderkop gave "Stierkampf" a generous spread of four pages of photographs, eight action pictures of Spanish and Portuguese bullfights. One, entitled *El Gallo's letzter Kampf,* is acknowledged as "Photo Jean Cocteau"; although Cocteau was one of Hemingway's antipathies, he was a valued contributor to Wedderkop, and the shot of the wounded matador was a most suitable illustration for "Stierkampf." Facing Cocteau's shot, another, entitled *Ein kritischer Moment,* is acknowledged as "Photo Hemmingway"; from the look of things, the scene is the Navarrese bullring in Pamplona. Still another shot, entitled *"A las vaccas." Kühe, die den Stier hinaus begleiten, der nicht kämpfen will,* is also acknowledged as "Photo Hemmingway"; Hemingway had caught a bull in a Ferdinandish moment. Taking the story and the elaborate display of photographs together, one comes to understand that Wedderkop's witholding "Stierkampf" from publication until June and July 1925 was due not so much to problems of translation as to its topicality. He wished to run it as a commentary on the Pamplona fair of 1925. And so it was: Hemingway and his friends attended the 1925 *feria;* Hemingway utilized their quarrels and love-making for the action of the central episode of *The Sun Also Rises;* and in his memoir *The Way It Was,* Harold Loeb furnished the biographical context of the novel. Wedderkop was indeed an extraordinarily able editor.

"The Undefeated" thus was accepted for publication in a German version before it was accepted for publication in the original English. (Not until March 1926 did a French translation appear, in the Parisian literary journal *Navire d'argent,* as "L'Invincible.") *The Dial* returned Hemingway's rejected Spanish story to him at Schruns. He came back to Paris in March 1925, and from there on March 27 he mailed a copy of "The Undefeated" to an acquaintance, the American poet Ernest Walsh. Walsh and a young Englishwoman, Ethel Moorhead, were then planning a new literary quarterly; they were to be coeditors, and Miss Moorhead was backing the venture with her own money. They named their prospective magazine *This Quarter,* in a punning recognition of its planned periodicity and also in honor of the artists' quarter, the Quartier Latin. It is doubtful that Hemingway's story sent from *The Dial* would have reached him in Schruns in two weeks or less. Dubious about the delay in receiving Alyse Gregory's verdict, he may have sent Walsh "The Undefeated" in hope of a reward beyond the mere publication of the story; admittedly this reasoning assumes that the second story Hemingway submitted to *The Dial* was "The Undefeated," and it may not have been. For most of the spring Hemingway expended considerable time and energy helping Walsh and Miss Moorhead with the details of the first issue of *This Quarter;* Hemingway's famous Nick Adams story, "Big Two-Hearted River," appeared in the first issue, for Spring 1925, and "The Undefeated" appeared in the second issue, for the fall and winter of 1925-26. The delay in first publishing "The Undefeated" in a journal may account for the fact that it was not included in the New York edition of *In Our Time* but instead was collected in *Men Without Women,* which Scribner published in 1927.

After Ernest Walsh's death, Ezra Pound remarked to

Harriet Monroe that he had his merits and probably knew his time was short — and that, also, in the midst of his farragos he occasionally said something amusing: "Tout ça a une valeur." Pound's kindness to the deceased reflects Walsh's admiration of him; the first issue of *This Quarter* was dedicated to "*Ezra Pound* who by his creative work, his editorship of several magazines, his helpful friendship for young and unknown artists, his many and untiring efforts to win better appreciation of what is firstrate in art comes first to our mind as meriting the gratitude of this dedication." The issue led off with Gertrude Stein's "Capital Capitals," later set to music by Virgil Thompson, and while it narcissistically included Walsh's own "Seventeen Poems," the other contributors included Kay Boyle (making her literary debut), Yvor Winters, H. D., Bryher, William Carlos Williams, Robert McAlmon, Harold Loeb, and Lewis Galantière. Hemingway's "Big Two-Hearted River" is probably the masterpiece of the collection. Besides his story, he contributed with Ethel Moorhead (whose drawing of Pound was reproduced), Walsh, and James Joyce to a section of the issue paying homage to Pound. In imitation of *The Transatlantic Review*, there was an art supplement, which featured reproductions of Brancusi's work. In his editorial comment entitled "Journalese," Walsh made it clear that *This Quarter* intended to become a rival of *The Dial*, *The Transatlantic Review*, and *Poetry*, and the contents of the second issue bear him out. Added to the contributors of the first issue are Morley Callaghan, Djuna Barnes, Ezra Pound (whose "Cantos XVII-XIX" were printed), Kenneth Fearing, Carl Sandburg, James Joyce (with no mere page of tribute this time but an "Extract from Work in Progress," a real coup), and Hemingway (whose "The Undefeated" occupied thirty pages of the issue).

Not only was Hemingway a major force in the publication of *This Quarter* — both as an editorial assistant and a contributor — he also received a review in the second issue from Ernest Walsh for which a soberly appropriate term is "ecstatic." "Hemingway has always been ripe," said Walsh. "He began life as a ripe force. . . . There are lines in Hemingway's stories *that come at one reading them as if they had grown in the reader's heart* out of an old memory or an old wish to remember." In an unintended parody of the rhapsodies of lady reviewers in one kind of magazine, Walsh gushed that Hemingway "is one of the elect. He belongs." Hemingway's view of Walsh is decidedly not so flattering as was Walsh's view of Hemingway, however.

"The Man Who Was Marked for Death," in *A Moveable Feast,* recounts Hemingway's association with Walsh and *This Quarter.* The story portrays Walsh as dark, handsome, impecunious, irresistible to gullible women, and fatally marked, marked for death as obviously as a doomed hero in a silent movie. In the story, Hemingway, in the role of the narrator, portrays himself as equally impecunious but also, in his way, as gullible as the women who supported Walsh. After his first meeting with Walsh, Hemingway next heard from Ezra Pound that their mutual acquaintance the lady-killer had been extricated from Claridge's despite an unpaid bill, by some female admirers of poetic art and some young males also fatally marked. Next Hemingway heard that Walsh was receiving support, monetary and artistic, from a different source — this would have been Ethel Moorhead, though Hemingway gallantly left a gap in his account here — and intended to found a new little magazine, of which he would be co-editor, in the Latin Quarter. Hemingway continues:

> At the time the *Dial,* an American literary magazine edited by Scofield Thayer, gave an annual award of, I believe, a thousand [*sic*] dollars for excellence in the practice of letters by a contributor. This was a huge sum for any straight writer to receive in those days, in addition to the prestige, and the award had gone to various people, all deserving naturally. . . .

> This quarterly, of which Walsh was one of the editors, was alleged to be going to award a very substantial sum to the contributor whose work should be judged the best at the end of the first four issues.

> If the news was passed around by gossip or rumor, or if it was a matter of personal confidence, cannot be said. Let us hope and believe always that it was completely honorable in every way. Certainly nothing could ever be said or imputed against Walsh's co-editor [Ethel Moorhead].

Rumors circulated about the award to be made by *This*

Quarter, and shortly after Hemingway heard them, Walsh invited him one day to lunch at one of the finest, most expensive restaurants in the Boul' Mich' district.

"You know you're to get the award, don't you?" inquired Ernest Walsh, and he assured Hemingway, "You're to get it."

Hemingway informed Walsh, "I don't think I deserve it. . . . it would not be ethical," but inwardly he was remarking to himself that Walsh was a confidence man who was trying (for some reason never adequately explained in *A Moveable Feast*) to beguile a brother writer. The ethics of the matter, as Hemingway sardonically explained it in his memoir, merely involved the identity of the first names both men bore. So outwardly, he was as courteous to Walsh as Walsh was charming to him, and when Walsh began to hemorrhage from his consumption and had to leave Paris for the Riviera, he asked Hemingway to see the issues of *This Quarter* through the printers, a task made all the heavier by their ignorance of English.

One day, much later, Hemingway met James Joyce strolling on the Boulevard St.-Germain, and Joyce asked whether Walsh had promised the mythical award to Hemingway. The reply was "Yes," and Joyce acknowledged that he too had been promised it; they agreed not to ask Pound the question.

A Moveable Feast, then, indicates that there was no award. But there was an award. Or, at any rate, there was an impressive pair of awards promised by the co-editors of *This Quarter,* all quite frankly premised on two points: the generosity of rich donors and the eager reception of their gifts by *This Quarter* for dispersal to deserving writers. In their joint "Editorial" in the first number, the co-editors announced that "We have received cheques toward the sum of two thousand dollars or five hundred pounds to be given to the contributor publishing the best work in the first four numbers" of the magazine. The second number again sought funds for award-giving; this time the plans were even more expansive, and Walsh and Miss Moorhead solicited backing for an annual award of "five hundred pounds or two thousand five hundred dollars," plus another "annual prize of two hundred and fifty pounds or twelve hundred dollars to be awarded to a contri-

butor to 'This Quarter' with special reference to the youth,
of that talent and need which shows promise, as opposed to
absolute success, or enriching the civilization of this age."

The exemplar of all that largesse was, of course, *The Dial*.
The connection between the two journals was tacitly acknowledged in the second number, when the editors used Harriet
Monroe's review of the new magazine, reprinted from her regular column in *Poetry* for July 1925: "And from across the sea
it clasps hands with *The Dial* in the effort to slambang the
plodding world into appreciation of modern — or more specifically, modernistic — art." But there was a difference: for
all its promise, inadequate financing hampered *This Quarter*.
Ernest Walsh did what he could for Ernest Hemingway by
extravagantly praising the early stories and by printing two of
them in *This Quarter*. Besides publishing such opinions,
Walsh probably talked to Hemingway about the lesser prize of
$1,200 — hence Hemingway's memory of the Dial Award as
being for $1,000 rather than for twice that sum. At the end
of his life, Hemingway accusingly recalled Walsh's unful-
filled assurances as a confidence man's attempt to surpass the
real thing, in this case *The Dial* and its annual award to writers; and thus Hemingway compared *This Quarter*, to its dis-
advantage, with *The Dial*. Perhaps there was also involved
an older man's pique about the easy gullibility of a hungry,
ambitious young writer.

The succeeding issues of *This Quarter* were less glittering
than the first issues that Walsh had solicited and that Hemingway had helped to set up for the printer. Walsh died on the
Riviera, of consumption, and Ethel Moorhead eventually resumed publication of *This Quarter* and until 1932 edited it
alone. Hemingway meanwhile had dropped out of that particular picture.

In fact, his association with the little magazines was about
over. "Notes on Contributors" in *The Little Review* for
Spring 1926 indicates the reason: "Ernest Hemingway: The
indications are that Hemingway is elected to be the big man
in American letters." Perhaps at Margaret Anderson's urging,
perhaps for old times' sake, Hemingway contributed to the
issue his brief "Banal Story" which, with slight additions, was
reprinted in *Men Without Women* in 1927. Not a story but a
sketch, these two pages depict — through a sarcastic use of the

clichés of advertising — the banality and sterility of American life, as typified by the stories, editorials, and advertisements of *The Forum,* a prominent magazine of opinion of the 1920's. Hemingway contrasts American life to life in Spain, as typified by his great Spanish culture-hero Manuel Garcia, the matador known professionally as Maera. Maera's death and funeral were national events; popular lithographs were hawked among the crowds, and 147 "bullfighters" followed Maera's corpse out to the cemetery. The attitude expressed in "Banal Story" pretty well sums up Hemingway's code in his early work, and the sketch, with its scorn for the multitude and for the commercialism of American life, is quite at home in *The Little Review.* Its Spring-Summer issue in 1926 was a "Collection of Work by Some Young Americans — in Contrast with the Work of Some Young Europeans: Mostly French-Surrealists"; and the contributors included several of Hemingway's friends and enemies of former Parisian days — Malcolm Cowley, Gorham B. Munson, Slater Brown, Hart Crane (with "Voyages," I-IV), Tristan Tzara. But Hemingway had forsaken the Quarter, had forsaken the little magazines with their isms and cults and feuds.

He was preparing to conquer the fields of literature, and it was time to pronounce a valediction to the narrow garden of the little magazines. Like so much that Hemingway wrote, that farewell contained a sting. His gratitude expressed to Sherwood Anderson, in the spring of 1925, for having put over the publication of *In Our Time* did not hinder the writing or the publication of *The Torrents of Spring* as a satire overtly aimed at Anderson's *Dark Laughter.* In a letter of May 21, 1926, to Anderson — just a week before Scribner published *The Torrents of Spring* — Hemingway tried to prepare *Dark Laughter's* author for the shock by confiding that in the fall of 1925, he had written his satire in just seven days (elsewhere he variously specifies the time of composition as six or eight days) after canvassing *Dark Laughter* with John Dos Passos. The performance, explained Hemingway, was meant as a joke (though not a mean one), but it was absolutely sincere. Brother writers, like prizefighters, should not have to pull their punches on one another in the literary ring, and so he, Ernest, was only doing what Sherwood by rights should do were Hemingway himself to produce something rotten. It was nothing personal, had nothing to do with their friendship. If *The Torrents of Spring* were to prove ill advised, then it would show that its author did not know what he was talking about.

That tore it: Anderson did take things personally, even though Hemingway further explained that the young had to be very sure always because the show is really very tough and that a man wants to win all the time, but unless he knows everything when he is twenty-five, he does not stand a chance of knowing anything at all when it has had time to shake down and he is thirty-five. By way of reply, Sherwood Anderson protested that Hemingway wrote high-hat letters.

Then Hemingway displayed his impenitence openly: he wasn't sorry he had written *The Torrents of Spring*, the book *was* funny (a verdict a good many readers agree with), and moreover he had received five hundred dollars for the work. In fact, his previous letter to Anderson had been intended as an apology-in-advance, to explain why he parodied a novelist whom he had read and admired for a long time and whom he was about to sock in the jaw. But, then, neither of them had glass jaws, so presumably Anderson would withstand the roundhouse swings of satire. Portions of Hemingway's apology are confusingly phrased, portions are downright mean, as when he informed the older man that if some writer started to produce slop and received only encouragement from his fellows, then America would never produce any truly great writers. No doubt Hemingway was concerned that *The Torrents of Spring* would hurt Anderson personally and would cause a rift in their relationship. But to the end of his life he was consistent in his explanation that his own first novel was the right answer evoked by *Dark Laughter*, so terribly bad, silly, and affected was it.

He submitted *Torrents of Spring* to Boni and Liveright with the immediate and no doubt intended result that he was was relieved of his agreement to submit *The Sun Also Rises* to Horace Liveright. Boni and Liveright refused *The Torrents of Spring*, both because it was a "bad" novel and a savage burlesque of the firm's major author, Sherwood Anderson; Hemingway sent it on to Scribner, and Scribner, by publishing it, secured Hemingway for life. In the novel, *The Dial* and H. L. Mencken's new *American Mercury,* published by Alfred A. Knopf, received due mention, as did other American and British periodicals. At one point, Yogi Johnson, a principal character remarks: "Scofield Thayer was my best man. I'm a Harvard man." As Yogi Johnson is a comically disheveled and disreputable person, the dig at Thayer's taste is obvious: with Watson, he had bestowed the Dial Award on Anderson.

A second passage also indicates Hemingway's feelings about *The Dial* and its contributors, when the wife of the other principal male character, Scripps O'Neil, is given a stream-of-thought passage in Anderson's manner: "Scripps going down slowly to work in the pump-factory in the mornings. Mrs. Scripps looking out of the window and watching him go up the street. Not much time for reading *The [Manchester] Guardian* now. Not much time for reading about English politics. Not much time for worrying about the cabinet crises over there in France. The French were a strange people. Joan of Arc. Eva le Gallienne. Clemenceau. Georges Carpentier. Sacha Guitry. Yvonne Printemps. Grock. Les Fratellinis. Gilbert Seldes. *The Dial*. The *Dial* Prize. Marianne Moore. E. E. Cummings. 'The Enormous Room.' 'Vanity Fair.' Frank Crowninshield. What was it all about? Where was it taking her?"

As Mrs. O'Neil is a waitress, one of Sherwood Anderson's little people, the satirical intention in portraying her as an *avant-garde* intellectual is obvious. The journalistic and tutorial associations of "Scripps" and "O'Neil" are equally clear to see. The string of names includes a fairly sizable group of persons whom, for one reason or another, Hemingway disliked, not so much the actors and actresses as the editors of *The Dial* and *Vanity Fair*, who had rejected his contributions. Some of the French names — Carpentier the boxer, followed by Sacha Guitry and Yvonne Printemps (Parisian actors, then man and wife), and the circus clowns and acrobats (Grock and Les Fratellinis) — bring to mind Gilbert Seldes. He had to be polished off because he had been managing editor of *The Dial*; his name by a process of association followed upon those of Grock and Les Fratellinis because in his book *The Seven Lively Arts*, Seldes had tried to bring together the fine arts and the popular arts of the music hall, the circus, and the comic strip. Seldes' book had been serialized

in both *The Dial and Vanity Fair,* and Hemingway's friend
Lewis Galantière had given it a mixed notice in *The Transatlantic Review.* Marianne Moore, whose vote had been
decisive in the rejection of Hemingway's Spanish story, received the Dial Award for 1924 and was now editing the
magazine. E. E. Cummings, another man Hemingway disliked, received the Dial Award for 1925; he had written a
widely acclaimed novel about the first World War, *The
Enormous Room.* Frank Crowninshield, editor of *Vanity
Fair,* had rejected Hemingway's satirical pieces, even when
they had been urged on the magazine by Donald Ogden
Stewart. Well, they all were now being paid back, in the coin
of Hemingway's scorn, the maunderings of Diana O'Neil.
Ford Madox Ford, D. H. Lawrence, H. L. Mencken, Gertrude
Stein, James Joyce, John Dos Passos, friends, mentors, enemies, their personalities, ways of speaking, and styles of writing were travestied in page after page; but the intense effort
of writing the novel proved cathartic. As Carlos Baker has
noted, *The Torrents of Spring* marked Hemingway's with-
drawal from the patterns in which he had spent his apprentice years.

EPILOGUE

WITH the publication of *The Sun Also Rises* in 1926, Hemingway summed up his beginnings with the little magazines. Even though Jake Barnes toiled for a major North American newspaper rather than *The Transatlantic Review* or *This Quarter*, his associates were the very men and women with whom Hemingway had worked after leaving journalism, whose contributions he had accepted, whose ambitions he had shared, whose friend and rival he had been. In this *ave atque vale* to the Quarter, he transcended their sphere.

He published no other important and significant work in the little magazines. True, throughout the 1920's and on into the early 1930's he made an occasional appearance, as in Eugene Jolas' *transition*, which in August 1927 published "Hills like White Elephants," one of the last of his stories to appear in the medium of the little magazine. To the Spring 1927 issue of Ezra Pound's short-lived *Exile*, Hemingway contributed a negligible scrap, "Neothomist Poem." His final appearance in any of the little magazines in which he had published his early work was in the December 1931 number of Ethel Moorhead's *This Quarter*, with "The Sea Change," collected in 1933 in *Winner Take Nothing*. But Hemingway's real farewell to the 1920's had been said over two years earlier, in the issue of *The Little Review* that was its farewell as well as Hemingway's.

In May 1929, Margaret Anderson and Jane Heap called it quits for their magazine and put out a number to which they invited their old contributors and some few friends as well to contribute. Rather than stories and poems or anything literary, the two editors asked for answers to a rather involved and quite personal questionnaire. The response, as might be expected, was varied. Otto Kahn cautiously refused to commit himself. Janet Flanner gaily and dutifully answered all the questions, responding to the first query as to what she would have liked to be that "I would like to have been a writer — to have been Sterne or any of the Brontes. I should like to be a writer — to be even Hemingway since he is better at being Hemingway than any of the other Hemingways," an interesting suggestion that by the spring of 1929 both Hemingway's style and his personal legend were being imitated. Janet Flanner had known Hemingway before his fame; she had lent him the two first thrillers by Georges Simenon that he ever read, and the legend did not awe her.

Hemingway's reply was not to the questionnaire but to the news of the discontinuance of *The Little Review*: he sent a "piece for the Final Number of yr. esteemed weekly," hoped that it would meet with the editorial qualifications "that it should not be literature," and concluded by asking for an acknowledgement of the receipt of his poetic "Valentine," wishing to learn whether it would be used "as there is a great demand for my work by the Atlantic Monthly and kindred periodicals and wd. not like to disappoint these editors when I have a piece so eminently or emminently saleable." Hemingway had, of course, published his story "Fifty Grand" in the *Atlantic* for July 1927, in the year that marked his entry into the major, conservative journals; the joke was that his "Valentine" to Margaret and Jane was another of his "obscene" poems and thus quite unsaleable to the *Atlantic* or *Scribner's*. But the gaminess of the verbiage and the sentiments was redeemed by the accompanying photograph, Helen Breaker's handsome chiaroscuro portrait of Hemingway as the Quarter had known him — in open-necked shirt, cap, and sweater.

There remained, however, one decidedly bitter after-
tatse of the period in the 1920's when Hemingway tried so
hard to seek for acceptance in the little magazines; his relations with *The Dial* and its with Hemingway remained trou-
bled. With the rapid fame that came to him, Hemingway
might have expected praise from *The Dial,* as an honorable
amends for its earlier rejections. He received mixed notices
from it, instead. Its brief review of his first popular success
was placed among the unsigned one-paragraph notices of the
"Briefer Mention" in the issue for January 1927, a surprising
miscalculation of a novel that set an enduring fashion, perhaps the enduring fashion in modern American fiction of the
naturalistic persuasion:

> If to report correctly and endlessly the vapid
> talk and indolent thinking of Montparnasse café
> idlers is to write a novel, Mr Hemingway has written
> a novel. His characters are as shallow as the saucers
> in which they stack their daily emotions [as much a
> thrust at *The Dial's* old associate, Harold Stearns, as
> at Hemingway's intentions], and instead of inter-
> preting his material — or even challenging it — he
> has been content merely to make a carbon copy of
> a not particularly significant surface of life in Paris.
> "Mike was a bad drunk. Brett was a good drunk.
> Bill was a good drunk. Cohn was never drunk."
> "I knew I was quite drunk." "It's funny what a
> wonderful gentility you get in the bar of a big
> hotel." There are acres of this, until the novel —
> aside from a few sprints of humour and now and
> then a "spill" of incident — begins to assume the
> rhythm, the monotony, and the absence of colour
> which one associates with a six-day bicycle race.

The New Republic almost immediately took *The Dial*
to task for such ossification of taste. Its column "A Number
of Things," in the issue of January 5, 1927, complimented *The
Dial* for awarding William Carlos Williams the Dial Award
for 1926 and praised the consistently satisfactory level of the
awards; then it went on to less pleasant matters. All the writers who had received the Dial Award "were represented in
the Dial during the first year of its present phase, 1920 —
as were most of its other important contributors. And it is

almost impossible to think of any interesting new American writer who has appeared since that time whom the Dial has encouraged. Yet, the supply of these charter contributors will presently become exhausted: with all respect to Doctor Williams, one is not sure that the prize-winning material of the Dial is not already beginning to run thin." What would *The Dial* do, asked *The New Republic,* "for deserving writers after another two or three years, if it continues as implacably as in the past to decline to interest itself in the original work of new artists?" Behind these rather general strictures Hemingway's shadow bulked large.

Sibley Watson — Thayer was *hors de combat* — took his time about replying to *The New Republic,* but reply he did. His editorial "Comment" for September 1927 attempted to define what constituted an "interesting new writer," and he declared *The Dial's* lack of interest in encouraging Anita Loos or John Erskine — though it had published "when he was a new writer" the work of Michael Arlen. "I have," said Dr. Watson, "great admiration for the healthy talent of Gordon Young whose melodramas in the *Adventure* magazine have been improving steadily for some years. And what could THE DIAL do for him?" Then, as Dr. Watson recently explained, "I apologized covertly to Hemingway . . . having just finished reading *The Sun Also Rises.* It seemed so good in the twenties — a well of uninhibited masculine sentiment"; and so there followed, in this "Comment," Dr. Watson's *amende honorable* for *The Dial's* rejection of Hemingway's work and for that dismaying "Briefer Mention" of Hemingway's novel: "Ernest Hemingway is another matter. His book, The Sun Also Rises, has more warmth in it than one is accustomed to find in a dozen American successes all together. Fortunately he has reached a level from which he can kick encouragement downstairs." In closing, Dr. Watson asked everyone to remember "that it is impossible in the world of letters to act or to refuse to act without stirring up a hurricane of catcalls, of which The New Republic's are not always the merriest. Lists of interesting new American writers of the past seven years will be gratefully received."

The New Republic refused to let *The Dial* get away with Dr. Watson's unsigned apologia. In its "New York Diary," under the title "The Decline of the Dial," *The New Republic* for October 12, 1927, replied at length and cited distinguished American writers who had emerged since 1920 whom *The Dial* had not encouraged, except to review their books favorably; in prose John Dos Passos, Ernest Hemingway, and Lewis Mumford were named. Miss Moore, said *The New Republic*, was not responsible for the recent policy of *The Dial*; from all that could be seen by a tolerably assiduous reader of the magazine, it was not a whit different under her editorship from what it was under Scofield Thayer's. The only difference appeared to be what was a genuine misfortune for its readers — that, now that Miss Moore had become editor of *The Dial*, she no longer published any poetry in it. In any case, *The Dial* needed somebody's attention; it was no longer serious. Whoever wrote this attack on *The Dial* must have had some inkling of the facts of the Hemingway-*Dial* relationship in order to make his point about the consistency of editorial policy at the magazine, though there he was accurate only in the limited sense that Miss Moore was bound by the extremely detailed editorial directives left by Scofield Thayer for her to follow. After all, Thayer changed his judgment of Hemingway's work; he printed Edmund Wilson's praise of *in our time* and urged the acceptance of Hemingway's story about bullfighting. It was Miss Moore who decided against acceptance of the story and who printed the disparaging paragraph about *The Sun Also Rises*.

The final notice Hemingway received in *The Dial* appeared in the issue for April 1928 — N. L. Rothman's review, three pages long, of *Men Without Women*. Rothman was a fledgling writer just out of C. C. N. Y., and his review constitutes a reversal by *The Dial* of its attitude toward Hemingway; precisely because Rothman was a new writer, he could without embarrassment express a different attitude in *The Dial* about Hemingway's work. Rothman's piece sets forth what amounts to the standard period interpretation of Hemingway's fiction: Hemingway had fashioned his "essentially courageous stoicism into as tragic and unforgettable a mould as one can find anywhere in American writing"; "there is no hope and no suspense in any of Hemingway's work"; there must be "no squealing, no quitting. Men must play at being undefeated. Consider Hemingway's short story of that title ... one of his finest"; "The Killers" constituted "high tragedy,

and high art"; as for the drinking ("How they drink!"), the
reviewer found "nothing so moving and tragic in its implica-
tions as that tired, almost mechanical ritual of intoxication,"
the only surcease for the characters of *The Sun Also Rises,*
"a temporary staving off of consciousness," which itself meant
"squarely facing an empty and purposeless existence." In the
last analysis, the closest one can get to Hemingway is that
"life is very much of a mess; that nothing can be done about
it; that we had best not talk about how badly things are really
going; that the only escape is in triviality that will consume
time, laughing or drinking, prize-fights or bull-fights." These
one may glean as probable of Hemingway's stoicism. "He
refuses to sympathize with his characters, and strips his stories of non-essential detail. . . . he could write a great tragedy.
He remains . . . our outstanding realist." The compliment
was great, but it came too late to help the cause of Hemingway or that of *The Dial.*

Despite the apology of Dr. Watson, despite the ensuing
compliment of N. L. Rothman, Hemingway regarded *The
Dial* unkindly for years. Dr. Watson himself noted "the recriminations that followed and still pursue us." The chief target of these recriminations was Gilbert Seldes. As early as
1924, in the August issue of *The Transatlantic Review,* Hemingway had mentioned the American dadas as being better
than the French and Roumanian dadas but as not knowing
"they are dadas, unless, of course, Mr. Seldes had told them,"
a reference to the popularity of Seldes' *Seven Lively Arts* and
its acceptance as a guidebook to the latest developments in
American art. Seldes was mentioned again, once more un-
favorably, in *The Torrents of Spring.* Not until the end of
1929, four months after the cessation of *The Dial* in July,
were there further recriminations. They came when Dorothy
Parker wrote a slapdash, gushy Profile of Hemingway in the
November 30 issue of *The New Yorker.* Entitled "The Artist's Reward," it portrayed Hemingway as irresistibly attractive: "in his early thirties, he weighs about two hundred
pounds, and he is even better than those photographs. The
effect upon women is such that they want to go right out and
get him and bring him home, stuffed." Miss Parker also
sketched Hemingway as an artist completely devoted to his
work and as taking such endless pains to get every scene,

every paragraph, every last word right that he rewrote the final pages of *A Farewell to Arms* seventy times — an improvement upon the versions that have the novelist achieving the same end by rewriting those pages only seventeen times (according to Carlos Baker) or thirty-nine times (according to Hemingway himself in an interview with George Plimpton). Dorothy Parker said that Hemingway was outrageously sensitive, "probably because his work had begot some specimens that should really be preserved in alcohol." After citing as such specimens the dismissal of *In Our Time* by *The American Mercury* and *Men Without Women* by an unnamed reviewer in an unnamed literary journal, Miss Parker added that there was "another young gentleman who once occupied the editorial chair of a now defunct magazine of culture, and sought, from there, to form the taste of the American public; he was shown some of Hemingway's work, then unpublished in the United States, refused it, and pronounced, 'I hear he has been a reporter — tell him to go on reporting and not try to write.' "

This vague and casual reference to Scofield Thayer was almost immediately taken up by Louis Sobol in his gossip column "Your Manhattan and Mine," for December 7, 1929, in Bernarr MacFadden's *New York Evening Graphic*: "Gilbert Seldes' letter to Ernest Hemingway turning down the latter's stories when they were first submitted to him as editor of the late Dial, and his advice that Hemingway give up trying to write and go back to the newspaper racket. Then Seldes' appreciative comments on E. H.'s books and his discovery of subtle talents that even Hemingway didn't know he possessed." Seldes wrote in protest to Ernest Hemingway, whom he supposed to be the source of the allegations, and received a reply on December 30, from the Palace Hotel Sanatorium of Montana sur Sierre, Switzerland, where Hemingway was spending the holidays. The reply was a denial that Hemingway had ever made any such accusations; Hemingway admitted having read Dorothy Parker's Profile and could not see why Seldes took exception to her mention of the editor of some now defunct magazine of culture. Why should that be Seldes? Besides, weren't all the magazines of culture defunct? What Hemingway did not know and what Seldes apparently did not point out in his protest was that Sobol had parroted

Dorothy Parker's carefully vague accusation and had proceeded to name names.

The incident is all the more curious because Sobol and
Seldes both were working at that time on Bernarr MacFadden's *Graphic*, the rackety tabloid that its employees and
others nicknamed the "Pornographic" because of its penchant
for sex and sex crimes. In one column, "The New Plays," Seldes
was the drama critic for MacFadden's paper, and when there
was no new play to be reviewed, he wrote another column,
"Second Sights," on whatever he found of interest. It was a
denial, however, not of Sobol's gossip but of Dorothy Parker's
ludicrous and garbled account that Seldes sent on to Hemingway; that is to say, before Sobol's item appeared in the *Evening Graphic*, Seldes wrote his protest to Hemingway.

The trouble was that the story of Scofield Thayer's rejection of Hemingway's early poems had been embroidered
by Dorothy Parker and that Louis Sobol had compounded the
error by making the wrong identification, choosing Seldes as
the villain of the incident rather than Thayer. By 1934, in
Hemingway's mind it was Seldes who indeed had actually
returned the poems with the gratuitous advice ascribed to
The Dial by Dorothy Parker and Louis Sobol. In September
1934, Ernest Hemingway wrote one of his "Cuban Letters" for
Esquire, this one entitled "Defense of Dirty Words." His
general thesis was that the writer must portray his metier accurately. His victims were the restrictions of daily journalism
and the magazines, and the boxing stories of Ring Lardner.
Writing in a daily paper or in a magazine, Lardner was restricted in his use of words; but when a writer publishes a
book, he can use whatever words he finds are necessary to the
accurate presentation of the people he is writing about if he
and his publishers will take the risk. By never writing a
dirty word in his boxing stories, Lardner distorted the language of the ring into a very comic diction, so that there was
no tragedy ever, because there was no truth.

To the November 1934 issue of *Esquire*, Seldes contributed a riposte to Hemingway's argument (and apology for his
own use of profanity in his stories). Seldes' "The Prizefighter
and the Bull" argued that what Lardner knew perfectly and
Hemingway "doesn't know at all is that these [dirty] words,
except in moments of peculiar stress, have ceased to possess

any meaning whatever, least of all a dirty meaning." It was not by distorting their language that Lardner robbed the pugilists of their nightly tragedy but by "observing them with less romance than Hemingway observes a sailfish or a bull." Hemingway was a great romantic writer who presented to the world a "series of magnificent unreal ideal characters upon whom we can hang wreaths and togas and all the other trappings of greatness." His people were better than life, more interesting, and actually inspiring. Lardner's people were not: "They are horribly like ourselves."

Even before Hemingway saw the November *Esquire,* he was protecting himself with the charge that Seldes had it in for him; he repeated Sobol's gossip that when Gilbert Seldes was editor of *The Dial,* Seldes had turned down his "stories." Seldes' advice, according to Hemingway, was that he should stick to newspaper work and not have any illusions about writing. Hemingway alleged, moreover, that he had kept Seldes' letter; and he displayed an arrived author's contempt for all those twerps who had turned sanctimonious as hell and were praising his work, because the cash would always be on the side of mealy-mouthed mediocrity and all they were praising was a Trend. The accusation and the alleged letter constitute one of those tall tales concocted by Ernest Hemingway such as have found a temporary resting place in A. E. Hotchner's ineffable *Papa Hemingway.* Nor was Hemingway's printed answer to Seldes — "Notes on Life and Letters" in *Esquire* for January 1935 — an answer at all so much as an attack on William Saroyan, then the latest literary discovery, and thus the newest rival. Hemingway disposed of Gilbert Seldes, at the start of the article, by remarking that since *Esquire* had begun to come out early each month, the early mailing was a break for those who could not wait a whole long month to get another shot of Gilbert Seldes: "it's a vice with me. I tried to break it off. They said all it would bring was blindness, insanity and death but I said no, I'd paid the fifty cents. I could take it or I could leave it alone. . . . Go on. Leave me alone. Let me read Seldes if I want to. It's no worse than a bad cold and if you get it at the start you can knock it with this stuff I'm going to give you. No man need fear Seldes any more. . . . There's no danger, men, as long as old Doc Hemingstein is in the magazine," and so on, the point being that Seldes had remained a minor writer who earned his living by writing about his more distinguished contemporaries, whereas Ernest Hemingway was the sort of contemporary about whom men like Seldes wrote their articles.

True, Hemingway by 1935 had no need to drop a name. Still, he was inaccurate in ascribing his rejection by *The Dial* to Gilbert Seldes. Not only had Louis Sobol twisted some gossip, but, in fact, the chronology implied by Sobol and the chronology of events do not agree. Six of the eighteen vignettes of *in our time* were evidently written between December 1922, when Hemingway's early work was lost in Paris, and the date when this initial *in our time* material was published in the Exiles number of *The Little Review,* for Spring 1923. The remaining twelve vignettes were written prior to the middle of July 1923, when Hemingway delivered the manuscript of *in our time* to William Bird. At the beginning of 1923, Gilbert Seldes left the *Dial* office for a stay in Europe and on January 9, 1923, sailed on the *Manchuria* for England. Once on the Continent, he worked for Thayer, helping to compile the folio of pictures, *Living Art,* and living on his stipend from *The Dial* for that chore, Seldes wrote *The Seven Lively Arts.* When he returned to America in September 1923, he resigned his post as managing editor, not editor, of *The Dial.* Incidentally, the editor, Thayer, preceded Seldes back to New York — and work at *The Dial* — in August 1923. Gilbert Seldes thus has been justified in denying to Donald Gallup and others that he ever wrote such a letter as Hemingway described, indeed that he corresponded at all with Hemingway in the period 1921-23.

That Hemingway laid upon Seldes the blame for his rejection by *The Dial* is understandable — if one takes into account the fabrications of the purveyors of New York literary gossip. He was acquainted with Louis Sobol and Dorothy Parker; the permutations of the Hemingway-Seldes story were no doubt partly the work of these two acquaintances, partly the creations of the central figure. There is another story, however, that although unspecified as to source, if true shows Hemingway was aware of Marianne Moore's role in his third and final rejection by *The Dial.* Once during the 1930's at a party given by Paul Rosenfeld, Hemingway telephoned Miss Moore and offered to send a cab to Brooklyn if she would come along and explain why *The Dial* had rejected his writing. He had heard she was responsible; she did not go.

To the end of his life and after, Hemingway vented his contempt for Gilbert Seldes, a contempt all the more mysterious for its unoffending object. Over a time span of almost forty years, the old hunter fired a final shot at Seldes — aiming at his review of *The Great Gatsby* in *The Dial* for August 1925! In previous reviews, Seldes had expressed not only a good many reservations but outright condescension toward Fitzgerald's fiction, such as *The Beautiful and Damned*, but now wrote that Fitzgerald's earlier faults as a novelist were not significant in *The Great Gatsby*, which "is full of faults," a fact that "doesn't matter in the slightest degree." For Fitzgerald had "more than matured; he has mastered his talents and gone soaring in a beautiful flight, leaving behind him everything dubious and tricky in his earlier work, and leaving even farther behind all the men of his own generation and most of his elders." Given his competitive temperament, Hemingway would not have responded to the comparison invited by Seldes' praise of a rival writer who had very recently also acted for Hemingway as a benefactor.

Hemingway was introduced to the review — appropriately entitled "Spring Flight" — by none other than Fitzgerald himself. He told Hemingway, it seems, that according to Maxwell Perkins, who had edited *The Great Gatsby* for Scribner, the novel was not selling well but had very fine reviews. Fitzgerald showed Hemingway a review by Gilbert Seldes "that could not have been better. It could only have been better," added Hemingway in a gratuitous aside to his readers, "if Gilbert Seldes had been better." The comment is one of the less appealing moments in a generally unappealing account of "Scott Fitzgerald" in *A Moveable Feast*.

Not the least interesting thing is that here as elsewhere in *A Moveable Feast* Hemingway made no attempt to put down *The Dial*. On the contrary, he wrote generously of it and spoke of its award as conferring prestige and as having "gone to various people, all deserving naturally." So one bitterness did not prevail. As for *The Dial*, in not publishing Hemingway's early work, it committed at worst a sin of omission, surely a venial one in contrast to the major positive achievement of the magazine that published and courageously advocated the work of T. S. Eliot, Ezra Pound, Sherwood Anderson, E. E. Cummings, William Carlos Williams, Marianne Moore, Van Wyck Brooks, and Kenneth Burke, *Dial* laureates all.

The enveloping jazzy hubbub of the 1920's vaudeville sounds faintly now, drifting away along the vistas of history, drowning in the cacophony of nearer and more imperative cries. The very distance lends a distinct atmosphere, a period charm, to the spectacle, enables the viewer to consider the actors in the haze of perspective as faces in a general scene and to listen to individual voices blending in the time's chorus. Framed in the proscenium of its decade, the story of Ernest Hemingway and the little magazines brings to mind Sibley Watson's admonition that it is impossible in the world of letters to act or to refuse to act without stirring up a hurricane of catcalls. For both Ernest Hemingway and the little magazines he first published his work in, the hurricane of catcalls has subsided. The players have absconded from their Paris. The revue begins to emerge as an entity, ripe for posterity's comments.

ACKNOWLEDGEMENTS AND NOTES

For the text of *Ernest Hemingway and the Little Magazines*, the major sources are the files of the little magazines themselves: *Broom* (1921-24), *The Dial* (1920-29), *The Double-Dealer* (1921-26), *The Little Review* (1914-29), *Poetry* (1912-   ), *Der Querschnitt* (1920-36), *This Quarter* (1925-32), *The Transatlantic Review* (1924), *Transition* (1927-38), *The Yellow Book* (1894-97).

Pertinent in Hemingway's writing for *Esquire* in the 1930's are his "Defense of Dirty Words," *Esquire*, II (September 1934), 19, 158B, 158D; "Notes on Life and Letters," *Esquire*, III (January 1935), 21, 159. Gilbert Seldes replied to Hemingway's piece in the September issue of *Esquire* with "The Prize-fighter and the Bull," *Esquire*, II (November 1934), 52, 175; and Hemingway's usual Cuban Letter ("Notes on Life and Letters" is the specific title) in the January 1935 issue of the magazine was his riposte to Seldes' critique.

That Ernest Hemingway submitted some of his early writing to *The Dial* (1920-29) only to have it rejected as unsuitable for publication has long been an open secret — one of those stories not generally known by the millions who read

his fiction but of abiding interest, nevertheless, to the relatively small circle intimately acquainted with the magazine
and its fortunes. It is also a story that has been distorted by
gossip and misinterpretation. Hemingway himself excused
his memoir of the 1920's from whatever strictures might be
made against its accuracy when he wrote, in 1960, in the
"Preface" to *A Moveable Feast* that for reasons that seemed
sufficient to himself, many places, people, observations, and
impressions had not been included in his memoir. Some, he
said, were secrets, some were common knowledge and had
often been written up and undoubtedly would be written
up again in the future. He concluded his "Preface" with
the caveat that if a reader preferred to do so, *A Moveable
Feast* might be looked upon as fiction. Still, Hemingway
opined, it just might be that such a work of fiction would
illuminate works written as factual accounts. In *A Moveable
Feast*, Hemingway did not mention his relationship with
The Dial. In view of his deliberate ambiguity about places,
people, observations, and impressions in the "Preface" to his
memoir, however, as well as because of what others have
said and written on the subject, an account of that relationship sets the historical and literary records straight, throws
some light on the background of Hemingway's early career,
and exemplifies the development of literary fashion in the
1920's.

I thank Charles Scribner's Sons for permission to quote
from Hemingway's *A Moveable Feast*. The edition of *A
Moveable Feast* used here is Bantam Books edn. (New York,
1965); pp. 3-6 ("A Good Café on the Place St.-Michel"), 13-
20 ("Miss Stein Instructs"), 25-31 ("Une Génération Perdue"),
43-45 ("People of the Seine"), 57 ("A False Spring"), 61
("The End of an Avocation"), 71-77 ("Hunger Was Good
Discipline", 83-84 ("Ford Madox Ford and the Devil's Dis-
ciple"), 91-92, 96 ("The Birth of a New School"), 107-17
("Ezra Pound and His Bel Esprit"), 121-27 ("The Man Who
Was Marked for Death"), 133-38 ("Evan Shipman at the
Lilas"), 151-52 ("Scott Fitzgerald"), 195-97, 200 ("There Is
Never Any End to Paris"), have been drawn on for back-
ground, for summary, for quotation.

The point of view with which Ernest Hemingway's early
writing for the little magazines has been approached in the

present book is that indicated by Ezra Pound in his essay, "Small Magazines," *The English Journal,* XIX (November 1930), 689-704; "Hemingway to all intents and purposes accepting the principles of good writing that had been contained in the earliest imagist document, and applying the stricture against superfluous words to his prose, polishing, repolishing, and eliminating, as can be seen in the clean, hard paragraphs of the first brief *In Our Time* [*sic*], in *They All Made Peace,* in *The Torrents of Spring,* and in the best pages of his later novels" (p. 700).

The correspondence between Ernest Hemingway, Scofield Thayer, and Alyse Gregory is in the Dial Papers now housed at the Beinicke Library, Yale University. For permission to use these papers, I thank Mr. Thayer's representative, Charles P. Williamson. I thank Mr. Donald C. Gallup, of Yale University Library, and the custodian of the Dial Papers housed there, Yale University Library, for making available the facilities for the use of these papers.

With the interest and cooperation of Gilbert Seldes, who suggested leads, wrote letters, and furnished papers from his files, I have written a more accurate book. And, of course, the late Alyse Gregory generously gave suggestions about her correspondence with Hemingway, even though in one crucial instance she was understandably — given the passage of well over forty years — mistaken. Still another correspondent, Dr. James Sibley Watson, Jr., provided facts of the Hemingway-*Dial* embroilment and gave his cool insight.

The portions of the text dealing with Hemingway's life are based upon Charles A. Fenton, *The Apprenticeship of Ernest Hemingway,* Compass Books Edn. (New York, 1958), pp. 94-150 (for the events of 1921-22), 251-63 (for some mention of later events); also see Carlos Baker, *Hemingway: The Writer as Artist,* 3d edn. (Princeton, N. J., 1963), pp. 4-9 (for the events of 1921-22), 24-34 (for those of 1924-25), and 249-66 (for "A Working Check-List of Hemingway's Prose, Poetry, and Journalism — with Notes"). And see Morley Callaghan, *That Summer in Paris* (New York, 1963).

For a different account of some of these events, see William Wasserstrom, "Hemingway, *The Dial,* and Ernest Walsh," *The South Atlantic Quarterly,* LXV (Spring 1966), 171-77. My narrative differs from Wasserstrom's with regard

to the number of times Hemingway submitted his work to
The Dial; the interpretation of Hemingway's poem "The
Soul of Spain," and consequently of Hemingway's relation to
Ezra Pound; the interpretation of Hemingway's remarks about
The Dial in "The Man Who Was Marked for Death," *A
Moveable Feast*, pp. 121-27; the relation of *The Dial* to *This
Quarter* when Ernest Walsh and Ethel Moorhead jointly
edited the latter journal; and the relations between certain
members of the *Dial* staff and Hemingway. Wasserstrom, pp.
172-77, bases a major portion of his essay on the assumption
that Hemingway's writing in "The Man Who Was Marked
for Death" "deliberately blurred" two separate magazines,
The Dial and *This Quarter*. The contention is untenable:
whatever his feelings about *The Dial*, Hemingway's few words
about it, quoted in the text, are eminently fair; he did not
confuse, deliberately or otherwise, the two magazines; his sole
target in "The Man Who Was Marked for Death" is Ernest
Walsh; and the case against Hemingway results from Wasserstrom's misreading of the text. One further point: Wasserstrom, p. 176, says that "even Pound, as that poem ["The
Soul of Spain"] shows, Hemingway chose as the butt of excremental verse." This too is a misreading, for Hemingway
wrote the poem explicitly to defend Pound against those who
disliked *il miglior fabbro,* as the text of my book explains.
As for Walsh, it is proper to echo Ezra Pound's words to Harriet Monroe (30 November 1926): "Poor Walsh. . . . After
all he came down on my head in *Poetry* . . . and he more recently annoyed Mr. Hemingway, etc. . . . I can't take it very
seriously. He had his merits and probably knew his time was
short. Also in the midst of his farragos he occasionally said
something amusing. Tout ça a une valeur." See *The Letters
of Ezra Pound,* ed. D. D. Paige (New York, 1950), p. 204.

See *Letters of Sherwood Anderson,* ed. Howard Mumford
Jones and Walter B. Rideout (Boston, 1953), Anderson to
Seldes (October 19, 1921), p. 76; Anderson to Rosenfeld
(October 24, 1921), pp. 76-81. For these events and an account
of the Dial Award, see Nicholas Joost, *Scofield Thayer and
The Dial* (Carbondale, Ill., 1964), pp. 60-73, especially pp.
64-71 for the account of the award to Anderson, pp. 166-70, for
the story of Pound's relations with *The Dial*, and pp. 248 ff.,

for the account of *The New Republic's* accusations that *The Dial* rejected Hemingway's early work.

Gertrude Stein in *The Autobiography of Alice B. Toklas* (New York, 1933), pp. 246-48, gives an account of the Pound-Stein meetings and, pp. 260-71, famously writes down Ernest Hemingway. Alice B. Toklas in *What Is Remembered* (New York, 1963) almost completely ignores Ezra Pound but gossips entertainingly about Ford Madox Ford, pp. 113-14. There is a curious discrepancy about the "tapestried" Picasso armchair and the little footstool in "petit point" (Toklas, p. 168) after a design by Picasso, stolen by the Germans in their retreat from Paris (of course the Maquis could just as easily have stolen the footstool). Were there two pieces of furniture so priceless in design and workmanship?

For Edmund Wilson's "Mr Hemingway's Dry-Points," *The Dial*, LXXVII (October 1924), 340-41, see the convenient reprint in Wilson's "Emergence of Hemingway," with relevant correspondence and commentary, in *The Shores of Light* (New York, 1952), pp. 115-24.

Other sources consulted are as follows, with page numbers specified as has seemed useful:

Adams, Richard P. "Recent Scholarship on Faulkner and Hemingway," *The Teacher and American Literature*. Ed. Lewis Leary. Champaign, Ill.: NCTE, 1965. Pp. 149-56.

Anderson, Margaret. *My Thirty Years' War*. New York: Covici Friede Publishers, 1930. Pp. 242-74, esp. pp. 256-60.

Anderson, Sherwood. *The Triumph of the Egg*. New York: B. W. Huebsch, Inc., 1921.

Anderson, Sherwood. *A New Testament*. New York: Boni and Liveright, 1927.

Anderson, Sherwood. *Memoirs*. New York: Harcourt, Brace and Company, 1942.

Antheil, George. *Bad Boy of Music*. New York: Doubleday, Doran and Company, Inc., 1945.

Beach, Sylvia, *Shakespeare and Company*. New York: Harcourt, Brace and Company, 1959.

"Bull Gores 2 Yanks Acting as Toreadores," *Chicago Daily*

Tribune, Tuesday, July 29, 1924, p. 1. [With a photograph of Hemingway.]

"Correspondence," *The New Republic,* XLIX (February 9, 1927), 332. [*The Dial* and new writers.]

[Connolly, Cyril, pseud.] Palinurus. The *Unquiet Grave, a Word Cycle.* New York: Harper and Brothers 1945. P.1: the first two paragraphs of Connolly's book are Hemingway's epigraph for "A Situation Report."

Cowley, Malcolm. *Exile's Return: A Literary Odyssey of the 1920's.* New York: Viking Press, 1951.

"The Decline of *The Dial,*" in "A New York Diary," *The New Republic,* LII (October 12, 1927), 211.

DeForest, Katharine. *Paris as It is.* New York: Doubleday, Page and Company, 1900.

Dos Passos, John. *The Best Times, an Informal Memoir.* New York: New American Library, Inc., 1966.

Elder, Donald, *Ring Lardner, a Biography.* Garden City, N.Y.: Doubleday and Co., 1956.

Eliot, T. S. *Collected Poems, 1909-1962.* London: Faber and Faber Limited, 1963.

Engel, Bernard. *Marianne Moore.* New York: Twayne Publishers, 1964.

Espey, John J. *Ezra Pound's Mauberly: a Study in Composition.* Berkeley, Calif.: University of California Press, 1955.

Ford, Ford Madox. *It Was the Nightingale.* Philadelphia: J. B. Lippincott Company, 1933. Pp. 259-371 *passim.*

——————. *Letters of Ford Madox Ford.* Edited by Richard M. Ludwig. Princeton, N.J.: Princeton University Press, 1965.

——————. *Portraits from Life.* A Gateway Edition. Chicago: Henry Regnery Company, 1960. Pp. 270-301.

——————. *Some Do Not.* New York: Thomas Seltzer, 1924.

Gallup, Donald, editor. *The Flowers of Friendship: Letters Written to Gertrude Stein.* New York: Alfred A. Knopf, Inc., 1953.

Gauvreau, Emile. *My Last Million Readers.* New York: E. P. Dutton and Company, 1941.

Goldring, Douglas. *Trained for Genius: the Life and Writings of Ford Madox Ford.* New York: E. P. Dutton and

Company, 1949.

Hecht, Ben. *A Child of the Century*. Signet Books edition. New York: New American Library, 1954. Pp. 217-18.

Hemingway, Ernest. *By-Line: Ernest Hemingway*. Edited by William White. New York: Charles Scribner's Sons, 1967.

——————. *The Collected Poems of Ernest Hemingway*. Pirated Edition. San Francisco: 1960.

——————. *Death in the Afternoon*. New York: Charles Scribner's Sons, 1932.

——————. *A Farewell to Arms*. Modern Standard Authors edition. New York: Charles Scribner's Sons, 1962.

——————. *The Fifth Column and the First Forty-Nine Stories*. New York: P. F. Collier and Son Corporation, n. d.

——————. "The Good Lions" and "The Faithful Bull," *Holiday*, IX (March 1951), 50-51.

——————. *The Green Hills of Africa*. New York: Charles Scribner's Sons, 1935.

——————. *In Our Time*, New York: Charles Scribner's Sons, 1955.

——————. *The Old Man and the Sea*. Modern Standard Authors edition. New York: Charles Scribner's Sons, 1962.

——————. *The Sun Also Rises*. Modern Standard Authors edition. New York: Charles Scribner's Sons, 1962.

——————. *The Torrents of Spring*. Introduction by Caresse Crosby. Crosby Continental Editions. Paris: Black Sun Press, 1931. Pp. i-vii, 44, 85-86, and *passim*.

——————. "A Visit with Ernest Hemingway," *Look*, XX (September 4, 1956), 23-31. [An interview by Hemingway, entitled "A Situation Report," with photographs the captions of which he wrote.]

——————. "Wanderings," *Poetry*, XXI (January 1923), 193-95.

——————. *Winner Take Nothing*. New York: Charles Scribner's Sons, 1933.

Hemingway, Leicester. *My Brother, Ernest Hemingway*.

New York: World Publishing Company, 1962, Pp. 88-99.

Highet, Gilbert. "Kitsch," *A Clerk of Oxenford*. New York: Oxford University Press, 1954. Pp. 210-19, esp. 217.

Hoffman, Frederick J., Charles Allen, and Carolyn F. Ulrich. *The Little Magazine*. Princeton, N. J.: Princeton University Press, 1947.

Hotchner, A. E. *Papa Hemingway*. New York: Random House, 1966.

Josephson, Matthew. *Life Among the Surrealists*. New York: Holt, Rinehart and Winston, 1962. Pp. 108-30, 213-42, 311-49.

Joyce, James. *Letters*. Edited by Richard Ellmann. New York: Viking Press, 1966. Joyce to John Quinn (11 March 1920), II, 460. II, 445, n. 1. Joyce to Ezra Pound (5 November 1920), III, 28-29.

Kramer, Dale. *Chicago Renaissance*. New York: Meredith Press, 1966.

Lania, Leo. *Hemingway*. New York: Viking Press, 1961.

Lardner, Ring. "I. Gaspari," *Chicago Literary Times*, February 15, 1924, p. 3.

Lewis, Wyndham. "Ernest Hemingway (The 'Dumb Ox')," *Men Without Art*. New York: Russell & Russell, Inc., 1964. First published in 1934. Pp. 17-41.

Loeb, Harold. *The Way It Was*. New York: Criterion Books, 1959.

MacFadden, Mary, and Emile Gauvreau. *Dumbbells and Carrot Strips*. New York: Henry Holt and Company, 1953.

MacLeish, Archibald. "Cinema of a Man," "Sentiments for a Dedication," "Voyage," *Collected Poems, 1917-1952*. Boston: Houghton Mifflin Company, 1952. Pp. 45-47, 83-84, and 88, respectively.

McAlmon, Robert. *McAlmon and the Lost Generation*. Edited by Robert Knoll. Lincoln, Nebr.: University of Nebraska Press, 1962. Pp. 184-88, 198, 221-40 *passim*.

Montgomery, Constance Cappel. *Hemingway in Michigan*. New York: Fleet Publishing Corporation, 1966. Pp. 190-200, 202.

Moore, Marianne. *Collected Poems*. New York: Macmillan, 1951.

——————. *Observations*. New York: Dial Press, 1924.

"News Notes," *Poetry,* XXI (January 1923), 230-31.

"News Notes," *Poetry,* XXVI (July 1925), 231-32.

"A Number of Things," *The New Republic,* XLIX (January 5, 1927), 192. [The Dial Award.]

O'Brien, Edward J., ed., *Best Short Stories of 1923.* Boston: Small, Maynard and Company, 1924. The dedication (to Hemingway), acknowledgement of permission to publish, and ascription of authorship of "My Old Man" (pp. 263-76) all are to "Ernest Hemenway."

Parker, Dorothy. "The Artist's Reward," *The New Yorker,* V (November 30, 1929), 28-31.

Plimpton, George. "The Art of Fiction XXI: Ernest Hemingway," *Paris Review,* No. 18 (Spring 1958), pp. 61-89, esp. p. 66.

Poli, Bernard J. *Ford Madox Ford and The Transatlantic Review.* Syracuse, N.Y.: Syracuse University Press, 1967. Pp. 58-59, 81-83, 102-26 *passim,* 129, 132, 141-43, 157, 163-65. Poli's account is essential but (as regards Hemingway) very biased; I found its details and sources helpful as regards Nathan Asch, Evan Shipman, and Krebs Friend.

Pound, Ezra. *The Cantos of Ezra Pound.* New York: New Directions, 1948.

——————. "Hugh Selwyn Mauberley (Life and Contacts)," in John J. Espey, *q.v.,* pp. 117-33.

Rascoe, Burton. *Before I Forget.* New York: Literary Guild of America, 1937.

——————. "A Bookman's Day Book," *New York Tribune,* Sunday, October 21, 1923, Part IX ("Magazine and Books"), p. 26.

——————, *We Were Interrupted.* New York: Doubleday and Company, 1947.

Reck, Michael. *Ezra Pound: A Close-up.* New York: McGraw-Hill Book Company, 1967. Pp. 40-41.

Sanford, Marceline Hemingway. *At the Hemingways: a Family Portrait.* Boston: Little, Brown and Company, 1962. Pp. 215-22.

Schevill, James. *Sherwood Anderson: His Life and Work.* Denver, Colo.: University of Denver Press, 1951.

Seldes, Gilbert. "Second Sights" *New York Evening Graphic,* Monday, March 3, 1929, p. 24 (review of Thornton

Wilder's *The Woman of Andros*). Seldes also wrote the *Graphic* drama reviews, e. g., "The New Play," Friday, March 28, 1930, p. 28 (review of *The Taming of the Shrew*).

Sheehy, Eugene P., and Kenneth A. Lohf, compilers. *The Achievement of Marianne Moore; a Bibliography*. New York: New York Public Library, 1958. Pp. 7-8.

Sobol Louis. "Your Broadway and Mine," *New York Evening Graphic*, Saturday, December 7, 1929, p. 29; for a representative column, see Monday, March 3, 1929, p. 25, facing Seldes' column. Sobol's daily gossip column replaced Walter Winchell's pioneering effort when Winchell departed from the *Graphic*.

Sprigge, Elizabeth. *Gertrude Stein, Her Life and Work*. New York: Harper and Brothers, Publishers, 1957.

Stewart, Donald Ogden. *Mr. and Mrs. Haddock Abroad*. New York: George H. Doran Company, 1924. [Illustrations by Herb Roth.]

——————. *A Parody Outline of History*. New York: George H. Doran Company, 1921. Part of the subtitle reads: "an Amusing and Satirical Picture of American Letters Today." [Illustrations by Herb Roth.]

——————. *Perfect Behavior: a Parody Outline of Etiquette*. New York: George H. Doran Company, 1922. On title-page: "A Guide for Ladies and Gentlemen in All Social Crises." [Illustrations by Ralph Barton.]

Strong, L. A. G. *Best Poems of 1923*. Boston: Small, Maynard and Company, 1924. P. 104: Ernest M. Hemingway, "Chapter Heading."

Tebbel, John. *The Compact History of the American Newspaper*. New York: Hawthorn Books, 1963. Pp. 224-26.

Toronto Star, 1922-24.

Wasserstrom, William. Untitled review of Nicholas Joost, *Scofield Thayer and The Dial* in *American Literature*, XXXVII (January 1966), 498-99.

Alec Waugh. "My First Publisher: Grant Richards," *My Brother Evelyn and Other Portraits*. New York: Farrar, Strauss and Giroux, 1967. P. 45.

White, Ray Lewis. "Hemingway's Private Explanation of *The Torrents of Spring*," *Modern Fiction Studies*, XIII (Summer 1967), 261-63.

White, William. "Hemingway: He Parlayed Journalism into Literary Fame," *Grassroots Editor,* VIII (May-June 1967), 12-14, 27.

Young, Philip. "On Dismembering Hemingway," *The Atlantic Monthly,* CCXVIII (August 1966), 45-49.

Young, Philip, *Ernest Hemingway: a Reconsideration.* University Park, Pa.: Pennsylvania State University Press, 1966.

Zukofsky, Louis. "Program: Objectivists 1931," *Poetry,* XXXVII (February 1931), 270-71.

INDEX